The writer and humorist, Patrick Campbell (1913 - 1980).

FLAGSTICK BOOKS

Edition of

HOW TO BECOME A SCRATCH GOLFER

By
Patrick Campbell

Introduction by Desmond Briggs

Republished by agreement with the
estate of Patrick Campbell and Ailsa, Inc.
ISBN: 0-940889-43-9

Introduction
by
Desmond Briggs

The Honorable Patrick Campbell, 3rd Baron Glenavy, sounds like a typical English aristocrat. Nothing was further from the truth; Paddy Campbell was born in 1913 into the prosperous Dublin middle class; his grandfather had been a very successful lawyer who served as the last Lord Chancellor of Ireland under the British Crown (hence the barony) and stayed on in the fledgling Irish republic's Senate; his father the second Baron - known to his son as 'the Lord' as in 'will provide' - became Governor of the Bank of Ireland. Paddy's mother Beatrice enjoyed many close friendships among the prominent writers and artists of her day - names like George Bernard Shaw, D.H. Lawrence, Katherine Mansfield, William Orpen and Jack B. Yeats - and, a well-regarded surrealist painter herself, her work still features in public collections throughout Ireland.

Against this Dublin background Patrick Campbell grew up, a late developer if ever there was one. He was past thirty when, by way of a column in the Irish Times, he got himself to London and found his role as a humorous writer. He had also, seriously, found golf. As he himself wrote -:

"It was the Lord, who loved all games, who introduced me to golf, but most of all he taught me to play it without reverence, to set out upon every round with a high sense of adventure, so that often we laughed so much that we were unable to play the next shot. I couldn't have had a better introduction to a game which many people treat almost as a religious exercise, a rite to be performed silently

INTRODUCTION

and devotedly, one in which laughter is blasphemous.

"Sometimes they have taken up the game because their doctors have recommended exercise. Sometimes they play it for business reasons, or just to get away from home. A lot of the time they're simply trying too hard to win.

"They make deadly companions on the golf course, where fifty percent of the pleasure lies in playing with the right people. The other fifty percent of the pleasure is divided between striking the ball properly and winning - but winning, of course, in a way that makes it seem one has scarcely been trying at all."

In the early '60s, Campbell was committed to writing two witty columns a week, and often contracted to film script work as well. In fact, many of his days drifted away on the lush golf courses of England's Home Counties: eventually, disgruntled or saddened editors found out, and in a short space of time he found himself unemployed. However, his reliable luck held, and he soon landed a column in London's prestigious Sunday Times, which was to be his corner, from which he looked out on his own bizarre, disaster-strewn world for the next eighteen years. At this time, I was a book publisher and, meeting Campbell through his agent, we had one of those long exploratory editorial lunches that ended with my company commissioning HOW TO BECOME A SCRATCH GOLFER.

It was at this time too that Paddy - lucky again - found himself television fame, first in the infamous BBC satirical shows hosted by David Frost, where his Irish talent for debunking the famous found a rich vein to tap, and then for many years on the quiz show 'Call My Bluff'

INTRODUCTION

where his gamesmanship, his zest for winning and his dry wit (not to mention his endearing stammer) earned him the affection of millions.

By now, I was Paddy's regular book editor, publishing the best of his work, including his autobiography MY LIFE AND EASY TIMES and THIRTY-FIVE YEARS ON THE JOB, an anthology of his best columns which I selected. We also became firm friends.

Paddy's best stroke of luck came in 1967 when he married Vivienne Knight, a fellow writer; she brought order, calm and happiness into his life, the more so when they decided to move permanently to the South of France, where Vivienne had a small Provencal farmhouse in the foothills of the Alpes Maritimes well inland from Cannes. Here, under the thirty-five gnarled and ancient olive trees they laid out an enchanting garden, installing a swimming pool and an allee for the playing of <u>Boules</u>, a bowling game which is played in the square of every village throughout France.

This time was the sunlit upland of Paddy's life, a time of generous hospitality to many friends, of good talk under the shade of the vines, and above all of much, much laughter. It has also to be admitted that at this time, Campbell gave up golf.

It was not a deliberate decision; rather, he was seduced by another sporting siren. <u>Boules</u> demanded the same competitiveness, the same deadly eye, the same coordination of the muscles as did golf: but he had no need to leave his compound, to walk out of paradise, in order to play. He could emerge, cooled down from the swimming pool with a pastis (a liquorice-based drink) in his hand

INTRODUCTION

and find in his own garden the game and the companionship he needed. The golf courses of the Cote d'Azur simply couldn't compete.

Patrick Campbell died in 1980. Vivienne stayed on in France for another thirteen years, tending her garden as she tended her memories of one who was, as the Irish have it, "a lovely man".

HOW TO BECOME A SCRATCH GOLFER

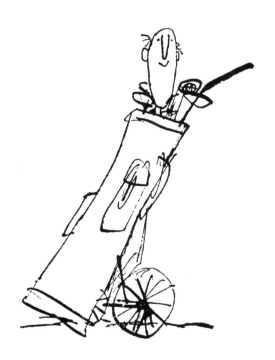

HOW TO BECOME A SCRATCH GOLFER

PATRICK CAMPBELL

Also by Patrick Campbell

CONSTANTLY IN PURSUIT
COME HERE TILL I TELL YOU
LIFE IN THIN SLICES
AN IRISHMAN'S DIARY
PATRICK CAMPBELL'S OMNIBUS
A SHORT TROT WITH A CULTURED MIND
A LONG DRINK OF COLD WATER

COPYRIGHT © 1963 BY PATRICK CAMPBELL

Library of Congress Catalog Card No. 63-21188

PRINTED IN THE UNITED STATES OF AMERICA

CONTENTS

1.	Fairway to the Golden World	7
2.	Keep Daddy out of Bounds	17
3.	Slide in Gently	29
4.	Kindly Do Not Tell Me—I Know	39
5.	Three down the Middle is Better than One on the Road	54
6.	Le Style, C'est Le Scratch Homme	62
7.	Practice Loses the Lot	77
8.	Muzzle the Rules—They Bite!	88
9.	Now No Good, Same Like You	101
10.	Cone Balls and Shrinkage	109
11.	The Big, Big Time	122

1

FAIRWAY TO THE GOLDEN WORLD

Arthur has just come down from one of the senior universities.

He has, in fact, come down rather sooner than his father was expecting, but Arthur isn't so surprised.

The place seems to be filled these days either with mere boys, so fresh from their grammar schools that study is still second nature to them, or with grown men, many of them wearing beards, who are working, as though earning overtime, for engineering or science degrees, while supporting wives and children in the outer suburbs.

These two groups have, as Arthur sees it, poisoned the minds of the University authorities by setting up and achieving work targets that might be admirable in underprivileged countries like Russia but are certainly uncalled for here, particularly as the University authorities are demanding the same degree of maniacal effort from everyone, regardless of their social position. (Arthur may have gone to the wrong college.)

Arthur comes down. His father asks him what he proposes to do.

Arthur, with the unsentimental, intellectual honesty of

the 1960's, says he doesn't know. He imagines he can either walk up and down King's Road, Chelsea, in his bare feet, looking for a job as a waiter in a bistro, or enter the family firm at the bottom where, Arthur estimates, he's liable to remain for the rest of his life, having no special interest in or talent for heavy engineering.

Arthur's father becomes angry. Arthur is being a fool. He will, of course, be joining the family firm not at the bottom but at the top, where he may be of some use to it, at a salary of £3,000 a year, plus expenses, on the promotion and development side.

Arthur becomes alarmed. Promoting and developing what?

Arthur's father, wondering at the sheltered life his son appears to have led, explains that Arthur will be promoting and developing business contacts, without which no major industry can survive.

Arthur becomes even more anxious. He doesn't know anything about heavy industrialists. He would put his capacity to interest or to entertain such persons at zero. What do they talk about? What do they do?

"Golf," says Arthur's father. "They play golf."

Arthur, he feels, in his child-like simplicity is growing more like his mother every day.

"You, too, will play golf," says Arthur's father. "Trade follows the flag-stick."

Arthur's father, who thought for a moment he might have coined a phrase, is disappointed by Arthur's response.

Arthur is merely amused. He is moved to the raucous, derisive laugh that has been annoying his father for years.

HOW TO BECOME A SCRATCH GOLFER

"Golf!" says Arthur. "That's the game for old women and cripples!"

He begins, in enthusiastic vein, to talk about Rugger, cricket and tennis, fast-moving, manly games at which he excels. "What's the matter," he wants to know, "with going in first wicket down for Surrey? That ought to bring in a good few orders for earth-movers, shouldn't it?"

Resignedly, Arthur's father asks Arthur to sit down. He'd hoped it wouldn't be necessary but the time has clearly come to tell Arthur the facts of life, or at least the ones that matter.

"Let us," says Arthur's father, lighting a cigar, "examine the social aura—and therefore the commercial benefits—of the three games you have mentioned, tennis, Rugger and cricket. Tennis, for a start, is out. It's a game infested on the upper levels with shamateurism, leading to working class youths staying in the best hotels. Even at Queen's Club persons are being groomed for stardom who do not have an independent income. Wimbledon, the Mecca of this so-called sport, has become an American slum with ex-ball-boys from Los Angeles making violent public scenes about decisions arrived at by British umpires of impeccable military antecedents, while the egregious Jack Kramer writes five figure cheques in the dressing-rooms. Furthermore—and this is the most important point of all—heavy industrialists, with the exception of Cyril Lord, do not play tennis. They may go to Wimbledon to look at the female players' drawers but this does not mean that they take any real interest in the game."

"Panties," says Arthur helpfully.

"Tennis," says Arthur's father, ignoring the correction,

"will not do. And the same thing goes for cricket. Cricket does have a certain social glamour, and consequently a commercial value, at such places as Arundel, specially if both Dukes are playing, but country-house cricket, with the opportunity for quiet business chats in the billiard room after stumps have been drawn, has largely disappeared. It's now a game in which the Players receive a disproportionate amount of publicity over such unpleasant controversies as chucking and throwing and the writing of offensive books, while the Gentlemen go unnoticed, unless trouble develops over the matter of wives on tour. Cricket, I regret to have to say, has slumped into being a Players' game, in a closed world."

"They're all the same now," says Arthur. "Gentlemen are players."

"The same thing goes," says Arthur's father with a shudder, "for Rugger. Like cricket, it's purely a spectator sport. No one over the age of twenty-five wishes to expose himself to the possibility of permanent injury at the hands of maddened London-Irish medical students, while the social life appears to confine itself to tearing electric light fittings off the walls in Midland railway hotels. Even the University match is not what it was, with persons in cloth caps paying to get in."

Arthur's father lights another cigar. "You will appreciate," he says, "my lack of compulsion to say anything about Soccer. What other sports do we have? Sailing? A matter of towing a twelve-foot plastic dinghy behind a Ford Anglia to the Welsh Harp. Socially, of course, Cowes, the Hamble and the Fastnet race are fairly beneficial but finance-wise you'll have to wait till I'm dead and by that time either another Labour government or the Chinese will be here, so the opportunity will not arise."

"What about the Russians, or the Americans?" says Arthur, indicating a certain measure of *Weltanschauung*.

"Swimming," says Arthur's father, paying no attention whatever. "Horrible. Public baths in such places as Ilford, Nottingham and Cardiff, where the leading exponents of the sport are mainly shorthand typists under the age of sixteen with virulently jealous mothers waiting on the edge with damp towels and packets of glucose. Hockey? Absolutely out of the question. A game for overgrown boys and, specially, overgrown girls, in which the acknowledged masters are Sikhs who play in turbans and bare feet. The social life of hockey pavilions I find unimaginable. Squash? A heart attack at thirty-one. Snooker? A diversion for bookmaker's clerks. Hunting, shooting and fishing? Admirable in themselves, but suffering from the same disability as yachting. Which brings me," says Arthur's father, a fanatical light beginning to gleam in his eye, "to golf."

"It's just knocking a little ball," says Arthur glumly, "into a little—"

"Socially," says Arthur's father, reaching for the 7-iron he always keeps behind his chair, "you cannot possibly do better, at reasonably competitive prices. Sunningdale, Gleneagles, Wentworth, the Berkshire! You're right in there with the men who count, and with a properly constituted fourball they can't get away from you for the best part of three hours."

Arthur's father drops a new golf-ball on the carpet. "A stationary ball," he cries, "which doesn't move until you

hit it, obviating all danger of being tackled or struck, or of having to run after it!"

Arthur's father lines up the wastepaper basket. "If you want to play Rugger," he says, "you need twenty-nine other players, a referee, two touch judges, a sodden field on the outskirts of Ealing and a chap to hand round the lemons. Cricket requires twenty-one other maniacs, two umpires, two scorers and a chemically prepared pitch which becomes unplayable after a light shower of rain."

Arthur's father lays his 7-iron behind the ball. "In tennis," he says, "if the other man is better than you are you spend half your time picking his service out of the back netting and the other half trying to get out of the way of his forehand drive. If he's worse the tedium is beyond belief. But in golf," cries Arthur's father, "you're out on your own!"

He flashes the 7-iron. The ball, aimed at the wastepaper basket, smashes a vase of flowers on the side-table. "The sensual joy," shouts Arthur's father, dropping another one, "of standing up there on the first tee at Sandwich and getting it slap-bang in the middle of the club-face and watching it rifle away into the teeth of a gale! Open that window, boy! The glorious open country you play over—no muddy pitches, no crumbling hard courts—in rain or shine, through woods or sand dunes, by lake and dell. Stand back, boy," bawls Arthur's father, "till I let one go!"

Before Arthur can take evasive action Arthur's father lets out a cry of Fore! With a full pivot, lateral hip-shift and wrists cocked till the last moment Arthur's father creams one clean through the open window into the rhododendrons on the other side of the drive. "And afterwards," says Arthur's father, holding a perfect finish, "in the bar, in the glorious camaraderie of golf, the unequalled opportunity to talk a little business far from the restrictions and suspicions of the board room. It's the finest game in the world!"

Arthur emerges from behind the door where he has taken refuge in case his father was thinking of doing it again.

"I think," says Arthur, "I see what you mean. Let's," he says thoughtfully, "have a swish with that stick."

"Gladly, my boy."

Arthur takes the 7-iron and lays the head of it warily on the carpet.

"No, no!" cries Arthur's father. "Not like that! You want to take the club in the left hand first, you see, so that the shaft passes from the knuckle joint of the first finger across the ball of the second, with the left thumb lying straight down the—"

Arthur's father—allowing, of course, for one or two unforgivable prejudices—has put the case for playing golf pretty well.

What he hasn't touched upon, seeing that he's been perfectly happy to play off fourteen for the whole of his adult life, is the extreme difficulty of playing it with skill, of becoming, in fact, a scratch golfer.

Before any attempt is made to drive off into the jungle country that lies ahead, it might be as well for us to define what we mean by this term.

What *is* a scratch golfer?

There are two kinds.

There is the man who, by artifice of style, clothing, talk and equipment, looks like one, but finds it difficult consistently to break eighty. Despite his aura of being scratch his actual handicap can be as high as four, to which he plays about twice a year.

There is the man who doesn't have to say anything, and can even play with the ends of his trousers tucked into his socks, but who goes round—every shot counted and all holed out—in seventy-two or less every single time.

The first is a scratch golfer in the company of elderly

players with handicaps of eighteen or, preferably, in the company of persons who have never seen the game played at all.

The second is a scratch golfer all the time, and is the one who gets the maximum pleasure from the game.

There is no need to believe people who say they play golf for the fresh air and the exercise, the ones who tell you they just like to give it a good old bash and never mind who wins, the ones who assure you that they go out in hail, rain and snow just for the fun of it.

All these people, every time they stand on the first tee, are expecting to play the round of their life. Pleasure lies in playing well, misery lies in scuffling it into the rough.

Count the number of times you've seen a man come bounding into the bar with this communiqué:

"Four large whiskeys, steward! I'm feeling really good. Topped m'first four tee-shots, three-putted on seven greens, lost two new balls and a fiver. What a splendid afternoon's work!"

Much more probably this is the man who trails in long after the others—he's been trying to gyp his caddy out of the tip—and stands around with a face like a wet afternoon at Datchet, griping about his lumbago, the condition of the fairways and the fact that this time the steward had really surpassed himself in the foulness of the lunch. He goes home early, looking forward to being bitterly unpleasant to his wife.

Count much more easily the number of times you've seen a man come into the bar with a quiet smile, courteously opening the door for the other players, modestly asking them what they'll have. All sensible persons, of

HOW TO BECOME A SCRATCH GOLFER

course, give him a wide berth because they can see that he's in a state of exaltation. He's bursting with triumph, because he's just gone round in sixty-nine. He loves the game, the course, the steward, the secretary, his caddy—but most of all he loves himself.

It so happened—and there is no method of preventing him telling you—that on the second tee he suddenly discovered, quite by chance, the ultimate, definitive secret of the game. Naturally, it has a personal application. He found he was standing too close to the ball. But by shifting back about an inch and a half, giving the hands plenty of room to come through, everything clicked beautifully into place and he hit a rasper right down the middle—the first decent tee-shot he'd hit in weeks. When he got up to it, however, he found it was lying a bit tight but he decided to go for it with his 3-wood and lo and behold—

His friends drift prudently away, leaving him to tell the rest of the heroic story to the barman, but he doesn't mind. He's in a state of grace.

Pleasure lies in playing well, misery lies in scuffling it into the rough. Let no novice, coming into the game for the first time, think it can be any other way.

How, then, can one become a scratch golfer, and derive the maximum pleasure from the most deeply satisfying of all games, while at the same time furthering one's commercial career?

The first and vital move is to go and watch the game being played by experts, before you attempt to play a single shot yourself.

It will be a revelation, such as came to the people of Israel, in January, 1961.

2

KEEP DADDY OUT OF BOUNDS

In January, 1961, an exhibition match took place between Sam Snead and Harry Weetman, to celebrate the opening of Israel's first golf-course at Caesarea.

It also marked the first occasion upon which a match was followed by a gallery of two thousand people only twelve of whom—by my own personal estimate—had ever seen the game played before.

A brisk breeze was blowing up the first fairway, touching at times, I should say, fifty miles an hour, as Snead and Weetman tossed for the honour.

Snead won, teed up his ball and then stood looking at the audience with an appearance of patience which anyone knowing him would not have trusted an inch.

What the audience was doing was commenting in Hebrew, German, Polish, French, Spanish and a variety of Scandinavian languages upon the force of the wind, the magnificence of the new club-house, the political situation *vis-a-vis* Jordan, Colonel Nasser and half a hundred other matters including Snead's Palm Beach straw hat. The babel of sound was tremendous, and only partially dissipated by the gale.

None of those present, of course, could have been expected to know that death-like silence should have been their portion, that Snead had been known to threaten legal action against people dropping pins half a mile away while he was trying to hole a four-foot putt.

As the Master continued to remain inactive, save for an ominous tapping of the right foot, the noise became even greater. I was able to identify enquiries in English, French and German as to whether he had already, perhaps, done it and if so where had it gone, and if he hadn't what was he waiting for and would it be possible for him to get on with it now?

Snead then made a suggestion which some of the stewards carried out in part, waving their arms and asking politely for silence. This had the immediate effect of redoubling the noise, people asking one another in genuine bewilderment how silence on their part could possibly contribute to whatever Snead was trying to do. In the end a comparative hush was achieved, Snead stepped up to his ball and with that long, beautifully timed, power-packed swing slashed one straight down the middle, quail high into the wind and all of 280 yards.

Deathlike silence fell upon the gallery, for the first time. They'd seen him hit it, but no one was prepared for the result. No one, in fact, had seen where the ball had gone. It had simply passed out of their ken and so they remained silent, rather than to appear at a disadvantage by applauding where, perhaps, no applause had been earned.

They were more ready for Weetman, as he stood up to it. Word had gone round that perhaps the ball went rather farther than anyone could have a right to expect. They saw every inch of Harry's tee-shot, an obviously apprehensive right-handed bash that took off like a bullet, turned sharp left and finished on the far side of the ninth fairway, about 150 yards off the line.

A great roar of applause went up, a thunderous clapping of hands. Snead's expression, never too sunny in action —or even in repose—would have frightened the lives out of a platoon of armed Algerian terrorists in broad daylight.

Subsequently, there was even worse to come. Many of the stewards got tired of the labour of lugging ropes around, seeing that the gallery paid little attention to them, and knocked off, leaving the ropes where they lay. At one moment, round about the seventh, Snead found himself trying to play a wedge shot over or around three

splendidly bearded old gentlemen who stood directly in front of him, watching whatever he was trying to do with lively interest. Later, a pretty girl in khaki shorts picked Harry Weetman's ball out of a bush and helpfully placed it in his hand.

But how, as I say, could anyone who had never seen golf played before know any better? And how can anyone who has never seen Snead hit a golf ball guess that that is the way it ought to be done?

It puts me in mind of the time I was playing in the Bowmaker Tournament at Sunningdale, partnered with Leopoldo Ruiz from the Argentine, who is popularly known as "The Thin Crust of Bread".

The Thin Crust is very tall, with shoulders a mile wide

and a seventeen-inch waist. He's incomparably the healthiest man I've ever seen and was feeling so healthy, indeed, on this occasion that he took to playing a 2-iron off every tee, in the interests of being able to find the ball again after he'd hit it.

He took his 2-iron off the fifth and with a punch so savage that his hands were over the ball while the clubhead was still about shoulder high he hit it 300-yards, almost beyond the pond, pulverizing the divot. There was a military looking gentleman, retired, standing beside me. "By God," he said in a low voice, "I've been playing golf for fifty years and I never knew it was supposed to look like that."

So let the novice, coming into the game for the first time, spend the first months of his apprenticeship following the experts and seeing how they do it. Then, and only then, let him turn his hand to trying to do it himself—under carefully chosen professional guidance.

In this matter there are two strict rules to be observed.

(1) Select a professional who really knows what he's talking about. There are several of them around.

(2) Keep all well-meaning friends—and in particular well-meaning fathers—away from the initiation ceremony, or you won't get a crack at it yourself.

I should like to illustrate what happens, if these two rules are ignored, by Case History Number One—an instructional method I have devised in preference to the more usual photographs of the author in action.

I've seen some of these. They would help no one except the author himself, and for him it's obviously too late.

Case History Number One will deal with Peter, a lightweight lad of sixteen, whose natural talents lie more in the direction of painting. Peter's golf-playing father, resisted all the way by Peter's mother, wants him to take up golf because it's more manly than messing about with Art.

Arthur, whom we have already met, would not be a suitable example in this case. Arthur, having already played cricket and tennis, will devise a swing for himself combining the leading features of the leg glide and the forehand drive and no professional will break him of it, ever.

Peter, however, comes virginal and unsullied to his work. There might have been some hope for him, if he'd kept Dad out of the way, but as it is ...

CASE HISTORY NUMBER ONE

Father is there on the practice ground for Peter's first lesson.

Not wishing to interfere with the lad's concentration, he parks the new, dark-green Rolls with the white-walled tyres under a nearby tree, to keep the sun off it, and sits unobtrusively at the wheel, smoking a straight-grained pipe.

Unfortunately, they haven't been able to get hold of the professional himself. He's away for the day at Sunningdale playing in a £50 a corner fourball with an American colonel and two wealthy garage proprietors, who are trying to get the filling station concession for the Base, so that the lesson is being given by the assistant, a lanky and not entirely competent youth called Dick.

Dick started to play at the age of eight, knocking stones

about with a cut-down jigger at the back of the caddy master's hut. He's got a long, smooth but slightly wristy swing, which comes to him as naturally as breathing. He is not exactly the stuff of which Open Champions are made because his long, wristy swing tends to get draw on all his iron shots so that in the summer, when the greens are hard, Dick spends a lot of time chipping back out of the heather and never with much success, as he finds the short game a bit fiddly.

Dick is, in fact, a little worried about his career. As things are going now two 69's barely get you among the qualifiers, and although it's no trouble to him to get round his home course in 66, specially in the winter when his iron shots often plug themselves quite near the hole, it's all rather different at Hoylake, Carnoustie and Deal, where if you so much as touch the damn thing on the green it goes skating about a mile past the can and if you're not to be packing your bag you've got to hole the long, slippery one back. And the same again at the next.

Dick has more or less decided that he'd better become a teaching, as opposed to a playing professional, but there's another difficulty here. He seems to have been born with his own long, smooth, wristy swing. There's nothing to it. In deep self-analysis Dick honestly can't imagine why other people seem to find it so hard. In even deeper self-analysis Dick also can't imagine what he can possibly tell them to put them right, though there is, of course, this malarkey about the right elbow.

This year the senior professional, now away at Sunningdale, is concentrating on the right elbow, as the ultimate secret of the game. (Last year it was the inward roll of the left knee, but even Dick realizes the commercial value of novelty.)

The senior professional, on the infrequent occasions when he's free to give pupils the benefit of his advice, makes them hit every shot with a handkerchief gripped in the right armpit. It's his trademark this year, and he insists, as proof of its effectiveness, that Dick's teaching bears the same imprint, despite the fact that Dick tried it himself once and got a quick hook so baleful that it took him nearly a week, having discarded the handkerchief, to hit one down the middle again, or as near to the middle as he ever gets.

Dick, presented with Peter, steels himself to face up to the whole rigmarole all over again. By the look of him Dick estimates that Peter has sufficient physical co-ordination to give him a chance, by exerting it to the full, of turning himself into a fair hand at draughts.

Dick begins to demonstrate the Vardon Grip, wishing that the pupil's old man were rather farther away—in some place like the bar in the club-house or, preferably, Bermuda.

The pupil's old man has, before now, taken Dick to task about his putting—the coolest piece of cheek, in Dick's estimate, imaginable—in view of the fact that the old goat can hardly hit a chip shot out of his own shadow.

Dick sincerely hopes that Peter's father will keep his distance, or he'll get into a muddle.

Ten minutes later Peter is locked in the state of rigor mortis natural to his first experience of the Vardon Grip.

"That's nice," says Dick. "Just try a swing. We'll see how it goes."

With infinite care, it's all he can do to move—Peter slowly lifts the stick into the air until it achieves a semi-vertical position, slowly brings it down again and raises it into a similar position on the other side. At the lowest point of the arc the club-head passes three inches above the ground.

As always, with a new pupil, Dick is stunned by the sheer paralytic hopelessness of it. It beats him, completely, why the ass doesn't just swish it back, shift his weight into it and flash the club-head through. He's wondering, as ever, where to begin on this mess when a loud, cheerful voice comes from the Rolls.

"Rather picking it up with the wrists, there, Pete, old chap. You want the club, left hand and left arm moving back all in the one piece."

Dick clenches his teeth. It's started. "Just try another swing," he tells his pupil. "Take the club-head back a bit closer to the ground."

Five minutes later Peter, having sensibly made his own furtive easement of the impossible rigours of the Vardon Grip, manages after three wispy air-shots to knock one twenty yards along the ground with a 7-iron.

"That's nice," says Dick. "That's coming." He remembers who, and what, pays the rent. "That right elbow's wandering a bit, though," he says. "If you cock up that elbow you're going to be outside the line going back. The right elbow," says Dick, "should be located close to the body until just after the moment of impact, providing a fulcrum to which the inside-out plane of the down swing can be anchored. You may find it helpful to place a handkerchief—"

"I don't want to butt in, but I think he'd find it easier to concentrate on a firm left arm," says Peter's father, who's strolled over from the Rolls. "Isn't it Hogan—or that other fellow, Max something—who says the less you think about the right hand the better? Give me that stick a sec, Pete," says Peter's father. "Of course," he tells Dick, "I can't quite get as far back as you young chaps—anno domini, you know—but surely if you take the club and the left hand and arm all back in the one piece—"

Peter's father makes the preliminary movement. He has a better idea. "Chuck a ball down there," he says. "I'll show you what I mean."

The first one nearly cuts the head off a man trying to hole a match-saver on the 18th, away to the left. "That's all that damn nonsense about anchoring the right elbow," says Peter's father cheerfully. "You see what happens?" he tells his son.

After the next one the four men on the 18th become convinced that a personal attack is being made upon them, for reasons beyond their imagining. They come together in a belligerent group, glaring across at their attacker on the practice ground.

Peter's father is oblivious to them. With a stiffer left arm than he's ever used before he's sliced three into the wood, in the opposite direction, and is now putting the whole thing down to a fault in his stance, or a premature transference of weight after the initial movement of the down swing.

"Watch this one," he tells Dick roughly. "I may be getting the left hip out of the way too late."

Peter, the novice, the learner, stands there with a great

HOW TO BECOME A SCRATCH GOLFER

weight on his soul. He'd thought, the first time he picked one up, that it wasn't going to be very easy with these long, heavy, narrow-headed sticks to hit such a small ball very far—or even at all—but never in his lowest moment had he guessed that the process was going to be governed by so many anatomical impossibilities.

Peter's first and almost certainly last lesson concludes with Peter sitting on the grass picking daisies in lacklustre fashion, while Dick tries to think of something—anything—that will stop Peter's father losing yet another of Dick's practice balls in the wood.

The instructions for the first lesson are therefore clear. Choose one of the deans among the teaching profes-

sionals, if you can catch him—a man hardened to the seemingly impossible chore of teaching a beginner, who yet retains a gleam of hope that it can be done.

Keep all well-meaning friends and fathers away, if you want to obtain the exclusive benefit of the professional's advice.

Thirdly, do not attempt to find out how to do it by yourself, or you'll build loops, lurches and irrelevant contortions into your swing—or whatever you decide eventually to call it—that will remain with you to your grave.

3

SLIDE IN GENTLY

The time has come to join a club, to buy a bag and the tools of your trade.

To become a member of a golf-club is a simple matter.

The requirement is:

Two members to propose and second you who are comparatively popular with at least 50% of the other members. They are not always easy to find.

Most golf clubs, as is right and proper in the friendliest and most sociable of all games, are well riddled with feuds and vendettas that keep the social life sparkling and alive.

Mr. A, for instance—one of your sponsors—has been behaving for years as though Mr. B did not exist. This coldness was created by an incident which took place in 1952, when Mr. B reported Mr. A to the secretary for bringing his dog into the locker-room, in flagrant defiance of a notice which used to be on the board, but which disappeared some time ago, clearly banning dogs on the club premises.

Mr. A's defence—a completely acceptable one to Mr. A and to the three other members of Mr. A's regular fourball—was that Mr. A, always a stickler for the rules, was dog-less in the locker-room when the dog—a notably loyal animal devoted to Mr. A—suddenly appeared, thanks to the fact that Mr. B had left the front door of the club open, ignoring a notice that said, "Please Keep Closed".

Sponsorship by the A group of the candidate for election may lead to him being black-balled, on the contention by the B group that if he gets in the whole premises will be overrun with dogs, leading to wholesale destruction of the furniture, thefts from the kitchen and additional work for the already over-burdened cleaning women.

There is almost no limit to the irreconcilable differences that can break out between the members of a golf-club. They are, furthermore, often so complex in origin that the original protagonists don't fully understand what the row was all about, while they remain determined to carry it on till death.

Mr. D, for instance, suddenly circularizes the members of his club with a memorandum, Roneo-ed by his office staff, that can go something like this:

Dear Members,

For some years I have felt that the existing records of our Competitions in the form of incomplete tablets on our stairs are not only inadequate but exhibited where they are of no value.

Regrettable as it is, there is a growing tendency to live solely in the present, but if there is anything left in tradition then surely it is of importance that our new, and particularly young members, should have some patent knowledge of these golfers—many of them of repute—who were once members of our Club.

I have, therefore, prepared a sketch of an Omnibus

Honours Board, which would be a gift to the club from myself.

I want it to be known that there are a few members of the committee who are against me in my proposal, feeling that there is no interest in studying the names of successful members in our competitions and there are others who think it would be a pity to do away with the existing tablets. On the other hand, I am by no means without support.

In my view, there are four possibilities that can be considered.

(1) Erect the board above the stairs (above where the tablets are at the moment) in which event there would be two supplementary boards—underneath the omnibus board—for competitions after 1960.

(2) Erect the board inside the main lounge—where there would be one supplementary board.

(3) Have no boards at all, but transfer the existing tablets (plus others to be printed for those competitions not yet recorded) to the main lounge, or to some suitable place where they can be seen.

(4) Leave matters as they are.

I should be grateful if members would record their preferences on the enclosed postcard, as the matter will be discussed at the next committee meeting.

Yours, etc.

An innocent and well-intentioned document of this kind can create bitternesses that will endure for weeks.

Members write to the Secretary asking if it is in order for the chairman of the handicapping committee, Mr. D, to attempt to interfere in matters which are the concern of the house committee, and if it is not what steps does the Secretary propose to take to put Mr. D in his place?

Another bloc votes solidly for leaving matters as they are. They do not pretend to understand what the practical application of all this stuff about tablets and omnibus and supplementary boards might be, but they do grasp very clearly Mr. D's motives in bringing it up.

Mr. D was runner-up in the President's Spoon in 1931 and 1932 and wants the evidence of his success to be placed in full view, where he and everyone else can see it.

Some of them have clashed over business deals with Mr. D, and feel it's just like his autocratic methods.

A third group votes to have the new board put up in the main lounge, not because they want it there, or anywhere else, but because they hope that the constructional upheaval may create a climate in which they can once again further their campaign for an extension of the bar, which everyone has known for years to be far too small.

The steward gets to hear about this move—in the way that he gets to hear about everything affecting his personal comfort and convenience—and starts lobbying to have the omnibus tablet, or whatever it is, put up above the stairs. The steward thinks the bar is quite big enough already. How many hands do the members think he's got?

The candidate for election, paying his preliminary, courtesy visits, is almost bound to get wind of all this dissension, as some of the members talk about little else and, rather than be branded as a pro- or anti-tablet man, with the attendant danger of being blackballed, may decide to postpone his entry until things settle down.

There is no point in this. As soon as the tablet business

is settled the question of whether or not the fire-place in the dining-room is to be blocked up will divide the members all over again.

The novice candidate, therefore, will do well to choose as his sponsors two members so unobtrusive that few of the other members known their names or even, in fact, that they are members of the club at all.

Most golf-clubs are eager for new members so that, provided proper precautions are taken, there should be little difficulty about getting in. The subscription ranges from five guineas a year up to fifty or more, but round about this top level a certain chooseyness is liable to break out.

The buying of a set of sticks should be left unreservedly in the hands of the club professional.

They can, of course, be bought on the novice's own initiative from a sports outfitter, but the professional's opinion of them is liable to be so low that the relationship between teacher and pupil will be permanently undermined.

Faced, for the first time, with the sight of the tools of his trade, the novice tends to disbelieve that so much stuff is necessary, and he may well be right.

A full set of clubs consists of a driver, 2-wood, 3-wood, 4-wood, all with leather caps, eight irons numbered from 2 to 9, a weapon called a wedge, and a putter. Fourteen clubs in all and at present prices the luxury article, plus a bag to carry them in, can cost all of £100.

They vary in weight and in the whippiness or rigidity of the shaft, but all professionals only have to take a brief look at their client to decide which combination is best for him. They always have it in stock.

As the novice's game improves he will almost certainly decide that the professional didn't know what he was talking about, and that the clubs chosen for him are ruinous to his game. Most professionals will agree, under pressure, that there may be something in this theory, and sell him another set, allowing him a certain percentage on the old ones.

No one, in these hard times, knows what becomes of second-hand clubs. They may be melted down or exported. Certainly, they are very seldom exposed for sale in the modern professional's shop.

In the good old days it was different. The pro's shop used to be cluttered with them. They could be bought for sums as low as half-a-crown, and probably went a long way towards retarding the beginner's progress. I know it took me several years to recover from the effect of my first set, presented to me free of charge by my father, who had been a keen player all his life.

In the belief that he would be glad to see a continuance of the grand old tradition I asked him, when my feet were first set upon the fairways at the age of seventeen, for a comprehensive set of new equipment, including a box of new balls. Well begun, in what I hoped would be our shared opinion, was half done.

He responded by fitting me out with what he called his spares—a quiver of implements as ill-fitted to their purpose as anything wielded by the Dutch in the early days of the game, when they were knocking stones about on the ice.

HOW TO BECOME A SCRATCH GOLFER

The full set amounted to four clubs, and each of them had a characteristic which made it worse than the other three. (When, later, I got my first matched set it seemed to make the game absurdly easy, for at least three days.)

The driver had a shaft so flexible that the head perceptibly drooped when the club was held out horizontally. It was called a Limbershaft. In action, the head seemed to linger behind at the back of the neck long after the hands had gone through and then suddenly come to life, like released elastic, whipping through the ball—if it didn't hit the ground first—with such uncontrollable speed that the shaft threatened to wind itself around my ears on the follow-through. When I really tried to hit one it produced a quick hook that would have bored a hole through concrete. A slower rhythm, giving the head time to catch up, was beyond my capacity then, and remains so to this day.

The driver made an uneasy stable companion with the 3-iron, the only other steel-shafted club in the bag. The grip on this was thin, hard and slippery, feeling on a winter's afternoon to be about the diameter of a knitting needle, and the shaft so rigid that a half-topped shot—a frequent occurence—produced the sensation of striking a block of granite with a double-handed axe.

I did most of my work through the green with the mashie, a club with which my father must have done a great deal of his work, too. Twenty years of wear and tear had bent the hickory shaft backwards in a gentle curve, so that at the address the hands were several inches ahead of the ball. Due, probably, to this malformation it was a club which could socket the ball at an exact right-angle to the intended line of flight. I was alone on the course when this mishap occurred for the first time and was so fascinated by the unexpectedness of it that I tried to do it again, and did. After that the socket became a permanent ingredient of my game.

Despite the fearfulness of these three clubs it was the putter, however, which was the real jewel in my diadem—a club so insane in conception that even my father, who'd bought it of his own free will, was never able to make a satisfactory estimate of the maker's original idea.

It, too, had a hickory shaft, with a red rubber knob on the end of the handle. The head was made of brass and was long enough to accommodate three balls at the same time, a trick I sometimes attempted from ranges as short as a yard, without any of them going in. It was no wonder that my father regarded it as a spare.

Fortunately for the novice, the manufacture of golf-clubs has now advanced so far that it is almost impossible to buy curios of this kind any longer. The modern weapon, indeed, is perfectly suited to its purpose. With a driver, a 3-wood, a 3, 5 and 7-iron and a putter, costing in the non-luxury article about three guineas apiece, the novice can set himself up for at least his first year. A small canvas bag to carry them in need not cost him very much more.

Later on, of course, these six basic implements will begin to seem hopelessly inadequate to give full expression to his increasing skill, and he'll burden himself with the whole armoury, stuffed into a duo-tone plastic bag with pockets large enough to contain enough clothing for a week at the seaside. A thoughtful analysis of the clubs he actually uses, however, will probably come out at the original driver, 3-wood, 3, 5 and 7-iron and the putter. Still, it's an aesthetic comfort to have the other eight clubs to hand and who knows but that some day, the ball fortuitously teed up in the middle of the fairway, it might not be possible to have a slash with one of them, with some measure of success.

So the novice has become a member in good standing, and fully paid up—thanks to the concession made by many clubs by which the subscription can be met by twice-yearly instalments.

He's got his own set of clubs, made—by the professional's assurance—to his own exact measurements.

He's also got the beginnings of a swing which, once in every five or six attempts, produces a shot quite like what he imagined it would be.

Golf has got him. Standing on station platforms he practices chip-shots with his umbrella. Under cover of his desk he tries to keep the left hand, while putting, square to the line of the hole. He carries his evening paper in the Vardon Grip, and cannot wait for the week-end to arrive.

He's ripe to start reading golf books.

4

KINDLY DO NOT TELL ME—
I KNOW

Mercifully, instructional books about golf are now written—with the present, notable exception—by acknowledged masters of the game, so that the average player can come to very little harm even by reading them from cover to cover.

The fierceness of modern competition, and the wideworld publicity which is given to success, guarantees that only top-grade professionals can rely upon a hearing.

It wasn't always like this. In the good old freer-for-all days any professional who won a major tournament could strike off into print, despite the fact that he'd won it by employing exactly the same method that had excluded him rigidly from the prize money for years.

He might, perhaps, have won the Open because just for once everything went miraculously right and the three quick hooks, to which he always helped himself when under pressure, this time bounded straight back into the middle of the fairway off a picnic party, a child's pram and a tree.

He might also have won the Open because he threw his own putter into a pond and, on the verge of hari-kari, borrowing a drooping, hickory shafted thing from the caddy master's father with which he holed them from all over the place in the final, thrill-packed round.

He could also have won the Open for reasons beyond his control. His only rival, for instance, standing on the sixteenth tee with five clear shots in hand, might suddenly have come to the conclusion that this was his year and so, to make it certain, he played a 2-iron instead of a driver, with the result that he finished with two sixes and a seven which would certainly have been an eight if he hadn't hit the stick with his chip, having socketed the two before.

This type of instruction manual, ghost-written for the new Open Champion by the Soccer correspondent of his local paper, was, however, not nearly as dangerous as the book written by the pure theorist, probably a teaching professional with an indoor, basement school. There is no need to remind experienced players of the havoc wrought by the American who published a book in the Thirties advocating a ramrod straight left arm throughout the whole duration of the swing. He succeeded in putting six strokes on to many players' handicaps in less than a year.

The novice, therefore, picking up his first golf book, should proceed with care. Although, as I say, they are written these days only by past-masters of the game, their teaching is open to individual interpretation which may well be far removed from the master's original intention.

This I should like to illustrate by—

CASE HISTORY NUMBER TWO

I played a lot with Major M— when I was new to the game, at the age of eighteen, for the reason that he was the only member of the club who had nothing to do from Monday to Friday either.

Being at that time a novice, I believed that anyone's play could be improved by a careful study of a book of instructions, and was working on this particular day on the full arc of the back swing, paying special attention to the need for a firm grip with the left hand at the top. I decided to pass on the message to the Major, who seemed to be in as urgent need of it as any man I'd ever met.

His method of striking was to bounce the shaft of the club on his right shoulder so that the down swing was initiated by a ricochet over which he had no control whatever, so that the ball could travel in any direction but never more than two feet above the ground.

The show-down came when he'd been bouncing the shaft with extra ferocity in an effort to hack a ball called a Goblin out of the pervading mud.

We played on a 9-hole course which consisted of three flat fields put together and divided by threadbare hedges, a venue offering little of interest to the power player except that it was downhill on a bicycle from where I lived. On this Tuesday afternoon, with an autumnal fog already settling in, the Major and I were naturally the only ones out.

It was at the short eighth that I asked him bluntly about the bouncing, an idiosyncrasy which had been weighing on my mind for some weeks.

It seemed a good time to deal with it, in view of the small, disused quarry on the right of the tee—the only feature of interest on the whole course.

We'd spent many hours in there already, poking about

in nettles, brambles and long wet grass for the Major's tee-shots and not infrequently, I had to allow, for my own as well, and though we'd inevitably uprooted or flattened a good deal of this undergrowth plenty of holding stuff still remained. Furthermore, I knew the Major was down to his last Goblin, and I had no desire to lend him one of mine.

"Excuse me, sir," I said, "it's only a suggestion, but have you ever tried getting your hands a little higher at the top of the swing?"

Up till then I'd only criticized the style of my contemporaries and so was not prepared for the reaction of an older man. The Major glared at me with a malevolence which was surprising, in view of my innocent desire to help. "You play it your way, sonnie," he snapped, "and I'll play it mine."

He bent down, to tee up his Goblin. He was, in fact, three-up, owing to a stiff-wristed putting method I was trying out for the first time.

The foliage in the quarry looked, however, particularly dank and uninviting, so I tried again. "But," I said, "you let your grip go altogether at the top of the swing so that the shaft bounces off your shoulder and ruins your arc."

"Arc?" said the Major. "Arc? Let me tell you something," he said. "Jimmy Braid always slackened his grip at the top of the swing and he'd have seen any of you young artichokes off any day of the week, wet or fine."

In later years I learnt, of course, that anyone over the age of fifty cannot be shaken in defence of his own swing, despite the fact that he's never played a medal round in less than ninety-three. At eighteen, however, I still believed that even the mature player would be interested in advice. "I know, sir," I said, "but I'm sure if you tried holding the club just a little more firmly at the top it would give you a lot more length off the tee."

"Ha!" the Major said, dismissing this sound principle out of hand. He squared up to his Goblin. He started his back-swing or, rather, initiated the jerk that normally lifted his mashie into the air, and all at once something looked different. His knuckles were shining white, indicating a grip on the club liable to squeeze the plug out of the shaft, if he were able to maintain it.

It was a phenomenon which was later to become only too familiar—that of the player who contemptuously rejects all advice on the grounds that it's drivel and then furtively tries to apply it, in case it might work—but I was too alarmed for the Major to consider it now.

He had reached the top of his swing—or whatever it was—and was standing on tip-toe with his left arm across his eyes and the club raised vertically in the air, presenting the appearance of a monk in plus-fours and a check cap about to haul down on the bell-rope for the opening chimes of the Angelus. Under the circumstances, it seemed improbable that he intended to continue with the stroke.

I was about to step forward and break the deadlock by taking the club away from him when he slashed suddenly and viciously downwards, making an attempt at the same time to turn his hips to the left, trying to deflect the clubhead from the vertical into the horizontal plane.

The result was something I'd never witnessed before, and have never been privileged to see again.

The head of the club buried itself in the mud nearly a yard behind the ball and remained there, leaving the shaft standing upright like a flagstick. It was not attended by the Major. The force of the impact had torn it from his hands. With nothing to hold on to he swung round, staggered forward and trod fairly and squarely on his Goblin, obliterating it from view. He stood there, facing the hole, vibrating a little and peering about to see where the ball had gone. Behind him, the mashie slowly keeled over and fell to the ground.

I picked it up, wiped some of the deposits off the head, and held it out to him. "That was bad luck, sir," I said, for the sake of saying something. "I think your foot slipped a little. Have it again."

He took the club from me, with a set face. He examined it briefly, as though to make sure it was his own. "All right, then," he said, "where's the ball?"

I had to hack it out of the ground with my own club. I teed it up for him again.

"If you wouldn't mind minding your own dam' business," the Major said, waggled once, bounced the shaft on his shoulder and slashed the ball straight into the quarry. I followed him immediately afterwards, out of nervousness. After poking about unsuccessfully for some time we walked in, the Major having run out of ammunition.

On the steps of the clubhouse he spoke for the first time since the quarry. "Interfering with a chap's game," he said, "is dam' nearly cheating, and I don't like it." He allowed the door to swing back in my face.

The inexpert player regards his own game as being, in fact, sacrosanct. He buys golf books not with the intention of remodelling his swing but merely to find the one simple hint or tip which will enable him to produce his normal game from his existing, paralytic method.

The inexpert player regards his normal game as being two shots below the par for the course, after his handicap has been removed, despite the fact that at no time has he ever broken 90.

Everyone who plays regularly has achieved par figures at every hole on his local course, but—naturally—not all at the same time. His score for the first five holes in the monthly medal may be 7-6-7-4-3. The 4 and the 3, where he holed a long putt at the short hole, he looks upon as his normal game. The 7-6-7 are aberrations, which could be ironed out by the one simple hint or tip which every new golf book should, but never does, provide.

It's this search for the one simple hint or tip which sells golf books, and the student has a wide field from which to make his choice.

Personally, I thought at one time that Ben Hogan had it, with his imaginary sheet of plate glass.

Hogan invited us to feel, as we stood up to the ball, that our heads protruded through a rectangular sheet of plate glass, the lower edge of which rested levelly on the ground just inside the pellet. By keeping, Hogan said, this lower edge on the ground we would get the idea of swinging back neither inside nor outside the line of flight but precisely in the correct plane.

It felt fine, standing up to the ball with the head sticking out through the hole and the sheet of plate glass there to check the lateral lurch and the whip round of the right shoulder that puts it through the Philpotts' greenhouse but unfortunately Hogan, ever the perfectionist, did not leave it at that.

As we came into the ball he asked us to concentrate upon hitching up the bottom left-hand corner of the sheet of glass so that the lower edge made an angle of about 12° with the ground!

Crippled by the complexities of the image, it was a fort-

night before I could get even a wedge shot into the air. The discomfort of hitching up that heavy sheet of glass with the tender muscles of the neck seemed to take all the steam out of the blow.

In studying golf books the novice would be well advised to pay more attention to the text than to the photographs of the Masters in action.

Photographs of Arnold Palmer, for instance, reveal that

on the down-swing his hips are almost facing the hole while his hands are about waist-high. Furthermore, his wrists are cocked so agonizingly that the head of the club is still somewhere up around the back of his neck. The novice, standing unclothed in front of the bathroom mirror and trying to reproduce this position even in still-life, unencumbered by a club, might well be put off the game for ever.

The verbal hint or tip is the thing to go for. It, at least, contains a message of hope, and gives the player the feeling that he is doing something different, even if the resulting blind slash looks exactly the same as it has always done to his friends.

I should like to illustrate the application of the verbal hint or tip by Case History Number Three.

CASE HISTORY NUMBER THREE

I used to play in a regular Sunday morning fourball with David F., a man who took golf books like cocaine in an effort to rid himself of a hook so virulent that the ball, on leaving the club-head, became almost visibly egg-shaped in its efforts to get round the corner, causing David to have to take a step back with his left foot in order to keep it in sight while it passed over the road.

When the toss of a coin condemned us to partnership I tried with everything I had ever heard about the game to bring about a cure, particularly at the second hole, a short one, where the tee was set back deeply in an avenue of trees, making it impossible for David's tee-shot to emerge into the open.

On one such Sunday morning I applied myself to his grip, it being the only physical feature of his game over which it looked as if he might have some control.

We had, frankly, become involved in a small game of cards—half a dollar ante and five bob jackpots—at his house the previous evening which had been interrupted—only, it seemed, a bare couple of hours later—by the arrival of his wife with breakfast, an intrusion for which she apologized. But then, she said, she couldn't have borne it if we'd been late for our morning round, particularly as there was so little to do about the house now that she'd got the children off to sleep again after the singing, or whatever it was, which had broken out round about dawn. Unless, she went on, we cared to stay to tidy up the sitting-room and in particular to shift the crates of stout which, even though empty, might prove too much for her strength, undermined as it had been by a somewhat sleepless night—

I could tell on the first tee that David, unfortunately my partner, had been more adversely affected than the rest of us, because he asked me if it was raining. It was, in fact, a hot still morning in July.

We lost the first hole to a 6. I was unable to take much part in it myself, suffering from the vertiginous feeling that my clubs had been shortened or the whole course lowered several inches by some outside agency during the night, so that even by striking sharply downwards I could reach only the top half of the ball.

David, of course, was in the car-park on the left with his tee-shot and picked up, after hitting the side of the pro's shop twice.

To stop the rot, before the opposition ran right away

from us, I had a word with him on the second tee, the one buried in the trees.

"I can't help you much," I said, "until my clubs get longer or the course comes up a bit, so that if we're going to get anything like a six here and a possible win you'll have to hit yours straight, or at least straight until it gets out of these trees. Try gripping very tight with your left hand and forget about the right altogether. I'll watch it for you, if I can see it. It's only thirty yards out into the clear."

He replied, as so many players do to helpful advice, by trying to defend his own method, one which, he said, he'd just picked up from a book by Henry Cotton. "I'm piccolo-ing my hands," he said. "It helps me to snap the wrists through."

"However the hell you piccolo," I said, "it snapped your opening blow into the car-park, from which you failed to emerge after two more."

He made a conversational detour, then, to tell me that my back swing off the first tee had put him in mind of an elderly woman of dubious morals trying to struggle out of a dress too tight around the shoulders. He was interrupted by the other two players, who said that they were both on the green and did we feel it was worth playing on?

I took, I have to admit, rather a quick swish at mine, jarring myself badly with a punchy little 5-iron which buried itself, after a very short, low flight, in the back slope of the ladies' tee.

It was David's turn. "Never mind the piccolo," I told him. "Just have a good bash with your left hand. If we're two down after this we can walk in."

He shaped up to it quite well, very relaxed, but leaning a little too far over the ball to promise complete control. Whatever he meant by piccolo-ing, I guessed it hadn't started yet. I was, in fact, just about to remind him that golf clubs had no connection with musical instruments when he suddenly played a stroke with a long, flowing arm action reminiscent of one of the supernumeraries in *Les Sylphides*. The ball passed harmlessly between his legs, but it was the other development that the rest of us found hard to credit. We turned back to look at the striker.

He was standing there with his hands held high in a good finish. After a moment, however, the suspicion seemed to enter his mind that all was not well. He lowered his hands slowly and looked at them. He examined the ground in front, and then behind. "Where," he said, after a short interval, "is my driver?"

The rest of us remained silent, looking at him with concern.

"My driver?" David said. "Where's it gone?"

"Why?" I asked him in the end. "How do you mean?"

He tried to put everything together, working on the available data. "My driver," he said. "I had it a minute ago, and now it's gone."

We turned to look at one another with mute enquiry. One of the other men said, "I certainly saw it in his hand just now. Perhaps," he said to David, "it slipped down the leg of your trousers."

"No, no," said the third man indignantly, "it's not there." He turned to David, speaking in a low voice. "If I were you," he said, "I'd move a shade to your left or it might easily fall on your head."

David acted fast, for a man in his physical shape. He sprang back silently, clutching both hands around his head. It was several seconds before he came to the conclusion that the danger, whatever it might be, had passed. He looked up cautiously, and it was then that we made the position clear.

"The hands," I said, "piccolo-ed through beautifully, but the club seemed to go on. That's it up there, near the top of that silver birch."

We sat down on the grass and lit cigarettes and for the next few minutes derived a lot of amusement from watching him throwing the rest of his clubs at his driver. Some of them got temporarily stuck, and came down at odd angles. Each time we gave him sharp cries of warning, to which he responded automatically, getting madder and madder. Someone suggested that it might be more economical of effort if he were to replace all the clubs in the bag and throw that.

David was in a bad mood when he eventually knocked the driver down, collected his scattered clubs and strode off towards the green.

We let him get to the end of the trees before we asked him where he was going.

When he came back we were sincere in our sympathy. His ball was lying in unplayably long grass behind, rather than in front of, the tee-box.

Afterwards I asked him what he thought he meant by piccolo-ing his grip. He demonstrated what he thought he meant. It looked interesting, the wrists cocked underneath the club—very similar, indeed, to the action of a man playing a piccolo. I tried it, got two screamers in a row and put the third one off the snout of the driver into a pond.

Conclusions to be reached from Case History Number Three.
Try anything once. It may enable you to play, for two consecutive shots, your normal game.

5

THREE DOWN THE MIDDLE IS BETTER THAN ONE ON THE ROAD

We may take it—and if we don't we won't be in before dark—that the novice has now advanced to a point of proficiency that enables him to get the ball into the air three times out of five, and once in every five times in approximately the right direction.

He should be well pleased with himself. Many people who have been playing the game for years are no more skilful.

We may also take it that until now he has played a complete round only with an equally inexperienced friend, or even by himself.

He still has to face the tensions of playing with strangers, to put his methods to the test of open competition.

It will be an experience which will give him an entirely new slant on the game, as illustrated by Case History Number Four.

CASE HISTORY NUMBER FOUR

Tom is eighteen years of age. He has been playing golf

for six months as privately as possible—that is, by himself and well out of sight of the clubhouse. Now and then, by his own estimate, he hits a really good one, but it's the other ones he would prefer no outside observer to see. Tom, who could do with a haircut, is sensitive to being laughed at.

He slinks out to the first tee on this Wednesday afternoon round about 1.30 p.m., when even the caddy master may be presumed to be having his lunch. Tom likes to knock it off the first tee with his 3-iron, hurry after it, give it another knock and then settle down in peace and privacy to his solitary round, and experimental work with his wooden clubs.

But this time two elderly ladies with small dogs shackled to their trolleys have beaten him to it. They're about a hundred yards away down the first fairway, having played three shots each already.

Tom tees up his ball—it's old and grey and not quite round—and stands beside it in a threatening attitude, inviting the ladies to let him through. He coughs ostentatiously, to attract their attention, but the ladies are oblivious to everything save their own conversation.

Tom tries an impatient practice swing and carves a surprisingly large divot out of the tee. Under cover of stooping to pick it up he shoots an apprehensive glance at the clubhouse windows, in case the secretary or, indeed, anyone else is watching, and sees three jolly businessmen advancing upon him. Attended by three caddies, they look like an army.

Before Tom has time to remove his grey, slightly ovoid

ball from the tee they are on him, inviting him to make up a four.

Old Ferris, it seems, has let them down. Old Ferris has so far lost his grip as to be unable to free himself, at ten minutes notice, from his business affairs to play a round of golf on this lovely sunny afternoon. "If you're on your own, lad," they say to Tom, "why don't you join us?"

There is nothing that Tom would rather do less, but short of going home there seems to be no way out.

"Tell you what, lad," says one of the businessmen—his name is Archie—"we'll take 'em on. What's your handicap?"

Tom has never had a handicap. "Ten," he says, feeling it to be about the middle register.

Old Norman, one of the other businessmen, whistles. "Bit hot for us," he says.

Old Fred, his partner, observes that Archie's fallen on his feet again. "Still," he says, "we'll have a bash. Dollar a corner do you?"

Tom nods dumbly. He's unable to estimate the size of his possible losses as he doesn't understand the significance of "a corner". If the worst comes to the worst, as it certainly will, he thinks he may be able to borrow a quid from the steward, if he can get him on one side for a moment.

Fred drives off, a typical, middle-aged businessman's shot off the heel of the club which passes over the edge of the rough on the left and comes in again, to finish about 150 yards down the middle of the fairway. Norman plays an almost exactly similar blow.

Archie is not so lucky. He tops his with a quick,

arthritic lurch, but the ball rolls fairly straight down the hill. "All right, lad," he says to Tom, "show us how to do it."

There is a curious silence after Tom has done it, although Tom calculates it to have been one of his better ones—a snoring quick hook that caught the down-slope of the neighbouring fairway and shot into the bushes behind the green at the short sixth.

"No need to bash the cover off it, lad," says Archie. "We're all friends here."

Archie manages to halve the hole with Fred and Norman, all three of them being down in seven shots without once leaving the fairway.

Tom's contribution is a socketed recovery shot out of the bushes which shoots off at right-angles, two straight along the ground with his 3-iron and a mashie shot which finishes in the hayfield on the other side of the road.

"You're bashing at it, lad," says Archie, on the next tee. "You want to keep it on the pretty, you know."

The three of them are straight down the middle this time, three very short, sliced bananas, but undeniably finishing on the pretty.

Tom has found an even older ball than the one he started with. In the interests of keeping it on the pretty he shortens his swing very considerably. The ball takes off like a bullet, strikes a tree on the right of the fairway, and rebounds almost to his feet.

"Well trained pellet," remarks Norman happily.

Archie is not so pleased. "You're just belting at it," he complains. "Swing the clubhead, can't you?"

It's the first time Tom has suffered critical comment

from a stranger or, indeed, from anyone else. It unnerves him absolutely. It makes him feel he isn't playing golf at all, but some childish game of his own invention. He tries swinging the clubhead. This time the ball misses the tree on the right by a yard and joins its predecessor in the hayfield across the road.

The silence which follows is broken by Fred. "If you can play down to ten," he tells Tom, "you must be really deadly with that old putter of yours." He's seen the instrument in Tom's bag, if not yet in use.

This privilege is granted to them at the next hole. Off the tee Tom's foot slips and he hits one 230 yards down the middle. He gets another skinny one with his 3-iron. It travels a couple of feet above the ground for another 200 yards and finishes in the far corner of the green.

"That's better, lad," says Archie. "You're getting your hands through better, now."

He, together with Fred and Norman, are on the green in four shots apiece, as usual without leaving the fairway.

It's Tom's putt. Downhill and a little slippery. Rather than dying away as it approaches the hole it appears actually to be gathering speed. It disappears over the opposite edge of the green into a deep pot bunker.

Tom fails to dislodge it with his first two attempts. The third one rockets the ball out of the trap, and once again into the hayfield across the road.

For the remainder of the round Tom is ignored not only by Archie but also by Fred and Norman. They proceed on their steady way, paralytically short but nearly straight, notching fives and sixes and not infrequently a seven.

Most of the time Tom is poking about in the trees, looking for balls. Several times he has to run to catch up with them, before they march off the next tee and leave him behind.

The thing that infuriates Tom very nearly to the point of tears is the utter hopelessness of the kind of golf that his companions are playing, and the fearful, smug satisfaction that they find in playing it.

He knows that if he could only hit two shots straight in succession he could beat all three of them single-handed.

At the long seventeenth Tom does hit two straight ones in a row. His third shot is another socket. It strikes Archie's caddy behind the ear—a miserable old man who up till now has been openly amused by Tom's efforts to keep up with the game.

Tom walks in alone from there, trying not to listen to the mounting chorus of complaint and derision, and determined to give up, now and for ever, a game at which only old and over-weight businessmen can hope to excel.

Tom, in fact, ought to be able to draw some useful lessons from this debilitating experience. Like the following:

(1) Young men with a fast, free-handed, open-shouldered action which is not, however, in several of its aspects classically correct, have to put up with too much purist advice from older men whose swing is not so much a swing as a spavined dunch, tending by its very paucity of effort to

keep the ball on the course instead of in the hayfield across the road. Young men should not, therefore, play with such persons until they're certain they can beat them six-and-five. Better to compete against one's equally open-shouldered contemporaries who can be relied upon to lose at least four balls per round.

(2) A six at a par-four hole which consists of three miniscule but straight shots down the middle, followed by three putts the last of which is shorter than a yard, is a more certain match winner than the power drive off the tee which turns sharp left and finishes up in an unplayable lie against the fence bordering Mrs. Arbuthnott's garden.

(3) Young men who, rightly, have no desire to play golf of this miserably pawky kind must devise a method of hitting the ball which cannot be criticized by elderly, over-weight business men—a method which *looks* as if it must achieve a certain birdie every time, and would certainly have done so if outside factors hadn't intervened—outside factors being broadly represented by the foot slipping, the caddy coughing, gusts of wind, sudden attacks of vertigo, business or domestic worries or—the most constant factor of all—sheer bad luck.

How, then, shall a young man standing on the first tee, and pretty certain that his first, second or third shot is going to finish in the hayfield, make it *look* as though he's a scratch golfer, when in fact he would find it extremely difficult to play to a fictitious handicap of ten?

One such artist is about to emerge from the clubhouse. Let us observe him.

6

LE STYLE, C'EST LE SCRATCH HOMME

The first tee on this chilly Sunday morning is in its usual state of tension.

The constituents of half a dozen four-balls stand about, swishing their drivers, waiting to get off.

They are all handicap players, and look like it. That is, they wear clothing specifically designed for the game. Zippered jackets with gussets let into the back to provide an easy movement of the shoulders. Rubberized, waterproof shoes, felt caps and hairy jerseys. Some of them, looking like post-operative lobotomys, wear white woollen hats with bobbles. Others have gone so far as to tuck the ends of their trousers into their socks. Nearly all of them have trolleys.

They are joined by a common emotion. Acute anxiety.

This is caused by the fact that they don't know from Adam what's going to happen when their turn comes to strike off—when they have to step up on to the tee and balance the ball on a peg and, in death-like silence, have a rigid waggle or two and then, rather suddenly, a bash at it, with everyone watching.

The north-east wind is making their eyes water. They

may not be able to see the ball at all, so that it will shoot off the toe of the club into the car-park where they'll have to rootle about for it under a lot of Mini Minors with the match behind them growing more and more restive on the tee.

Alternatively, they may hook it, as usual, into the long

and tangled grass behind the third green and lose a brand-new ball first crack out of the box while the next two matches play through, getting the day off to a jagged start from which it will certainly not recover.

Some of the fourballs have not yet been fully organized. They toss for partners and get the very chap they didn't want so that an argument develops about tossing again, on the grounds that one of the coins came down sideways.

No sooner is this matter settled than two of the players refuse to play for ten bob a corner, because they thought it was only going to be a dollar, so they have to toss all over again to decide this, too.

Someone, feeling his muscles stiffening in the chill wind, tries a practice swing and cracks someone else on the head with his driver. The apologies fatally interrupt a player driving off at that very moment.

Just as his partner is about to strike someone else finds his caddy is missing and starts roaring across to the caddy master, causing the man to top his drive.

In the midst of this nervous chaos the man who looks like a Scratchman appears on the steps of the clubhouse, and one sees at once how it ought to be done.

He is dressed, for a start, in a way which gives the on-looker no clue that he is going to play golf at all. Where the handicap men wear the muddy, shapeless slacks they keep specially for golf, he wears the trousers of what is obviously a very, very good tweed suit. They are narrow, immaculately pressed and carry, like as not, a beige overcheck on a darker, heather-mixture ground.

The beige motif is repeated in his V-necked, cashmere pullover, under which he wears a navy-blue shirt of fine

wool, tieless but buttoned neatly at the neck. The sleeves of the pullover are pushed up not quite to the elbow, lending the suggestion of a workmanlike quality to his otherwise casual air.

He is hatless. Some of the handicap men are wearing green berets, pulled down over their ears.

He wears a thin, brown leather glove on his left hand.

The few handicap men who wear them have chosen red, blue or even yellow.

The only real clue that the man who looks like a scratch golfer is about to play golf is to be found in his shoes. They are of grained, black leather, dubbined rather than polished. They have Norwegian toe-caps, with a raised seam, and are fiercely armoured with long pointed spikes, like running shoes.

Over his arm he carries a thin, buttoned cardigan, of the same beige wool as his pullover. He is in no hurry at all.

He is, in fact, in so little hurry that he pauses on the steps of the clubhouse to exchange the time of day with two pretty women whose husbands are already waiting for him on the tee. Laughter rings out. He leaves them, with the gloved left hand raised in formal farewell.

The husbands urge him to hurry. They're off next. He gives them a reassuring wave—and walks thoughtfully across to examine the surface of the eighteenth green. It takes a little time. He presses his spikes into the turf, making—one would hazard a guess—a test for moisture content. As he is about to walk away he stops and looks across the green, head slightly on one side. Facts—we imagine—are probably being correlated about the length and texture of the grass which may be useful for one of those awkward 15-footers later on. He concludes his examination with a slight shrug of the shoulders, indicating—we can only presume—that conditions are not nearly as good as they are, say, at a real course like the Berkshire, but will have to be endured. He joins the other players on the tee, to be greeted with a barrage of complaint that it'll be dark, if he doesn't hurry up and get on with it.

The Scratchman is entirely unperturbed. "There's ample time, gentlemen," he tells them calmly, "for all of us to notch our usual ninety-three." He looks round. "Where's my lad?" he enquires. "Or perhaps he's still in bed—"

His caddy steps forward. The Scratchman's caddy is always there before him. No shouting at the caddy master is ever required. "Morning, Jigger," says the Scratchman. "I hope you spent a quiet night. Sir's just this side of the grave."

Sir, of course, always knows his caddy's name—or, rather, the nickname by which the caddy is known from Troon to Sandwich by other caddies on the tournament circuit.

Jigger nods, without saying anything. He knows better than to try to get in on the act. He isn't, in fact, too stimulated by it, having seen it too often before. He only hopes that the news about Sir being just this side of the grave isn't true, or they'll be spending even more of the day than usual in the long grass.

The Scratchman ties the arms of his cardigan round Jigger's neck. "We'll keep that in reserve," he says. "The blood's liable to thin out just before lunch." Fastidiously, Jigger removes the cardigan and puts it in the bag.

"Well, now," says the Scratchman, "who's playing with what, and for how many?"

The other players, in an effort to get *some*thing moving, have already tossed for partners, so that Willy, the odd man out, gets the Scratchman.

Willy, in fact, owing to a habit of twitching his chip shots clean over every green, is absolutely useless off a handicap of fourteen. The Scratchman, however, appears overjoyed to have him as a partner. "The result," he announces, "is unclouded by doubt. We can only hope they save themselves a couple of shillings on the bye-bye. All right," he tells their opponents, "why don't you two top it first."

The opponents point out that it isn't their honour.

The Scratchman is surprised. He doesn't understand the complexities of handicaps, as he doesn't use one himself.

"Our honour?" he says. "Well, it's only the first of eighteen. Have a slash at it, Willy, while I have an attack of the shakes."

While Willy goes through the contortions that propel his tee-shot 125 yards into the rough on the right the Scratchman puts on a comedy impression of delirium tremens so acute that not even the experienced watchers can make an estimate of what he was doing the night before. The Scratchman fills it in for them.

"Pernod," he explains, "with tiny actresses. Never again, till tomorrow night."

Willy steps down off the tee. It's the Scratchman's turn to play, and all at once a remarkable change comes over him.

He becomes extremely serious. All trace of the earlier comic element is switched off. He throws his cigarette away—half-smoked—and mounts the tee, his gaze fixed on a point 300 yards away, down the middle of the first fairway. Slowly, he peels the paper off a new ball, handing the paper to Jigger, who resignedly drops it into the teebox immediately beside them.

HOW TO BECOME A SCRATCH GOLFER

Still looking at the distant target, he goes over to Jigger and rests a hand on top of his woods, in their leather jackets.

"What d'you think, Jig?" he says.

This is the part that Jigger can't stand. The first hole is wide open, and mainly downhill. It's more than 400 yards in length and no human being on the face of the earth could conceivably take anything else except a driver. Jigger starts to take it out.

The Scratchman stops him. "I'm not sure—" he begins. He comes to the big decision. "Okay," he says. "You're probably right."

He occupies the whole of the next half minute with a clinical survey of the ground, looking for the exact position on which to tee his ball, eventually choosing a site far over on the left. He tees the ball and puts the clubhead behind it. Delicately, like Menuhin at work on a Stradivarius, he eases his fingers round the shaft of the club, into the Vardon Grip. At the moment when it might be presumed—and many of the handicap men are deceived —that he might be about to settle himself to hit the ball, the Scratchman suddenly loses all interest in it. He steps away, holding the club out almost horizontally, he eyes once again fixed on the target 300 yards away. "Keep her leftish, Jig?" he enquires, very seriously.

Jigger nods. He wishes to God he was carrying for one of the other cripples who, if they can't hit it out of their way, at least do it quicker.

"Right," says the Scratchman. And at last he steps up to the ball. He looks really menacing. The jaw sets. He beds his ferocious spikes deep into the ground. He turns his head a fraction, to pin-point the target 300 yards away. Then he cocks his chin, so that it points an inch behind the ball.

It's the long-awaited signal—a gesture matched only in suspense by the officer in charge of the firing-squad raising his right arm. HE'S GOING TO DO IT NOW!

The Scratchman starts slowly back, club-head low to the ground, left arm and left side all in one piece. He hasn't the faintest idea what the result of the shot will be. Probably the usual whistling hook into the nettles behind the third where Jigger, as usual, will make hardly any effort to find it, so that it's the end of a new ball. About half way up the Scratchman takes a muscle-wrenching grip with his left hand, letting the right go slack. If only he can cut it, or push it, it'll finish up on the thirteenth fairway, where at least they'll be able to find it ...

He starts down too quick. His head comes up. With a single split-second to spare the club-head just catches the upper half of the ball, launching it straight down the middle, very low, but all of 240 yards.

"Great shot," murmurs the audience, who genuinely believe, in view of the ceremonial preceding it, that it was.

The Scratchman stoops to pick up his tee, using the opportunity to take a quick sideways look down the course. He's no idea where the ball went to. He lost sight of it the moment he started his down swing, and never caught a glimpse of it again. If anything, it felt hooky, and is almost certainly in the nettles. The Scratchman suddenly sees it, a white dot on the verdant fairway, a surprising distance away.

"Well," he allows, to the profoundly envious handicap men, "it's adequate." With apparent sincerity he commends the revolting strokes played by both his opponents, and then strides off, relaxed and easy, and already launched upon a conversational theme which has nothing whatever to do with golf.

The reputation he leaves behind is secure. It is, the handicap men agree among themselves, the concentration that does it. They could see, from the moment he stepped up on to the tee, that he knew what he was doing, that he had a clear mental picture of the shot he was going to play. And he played it. He *looked* as though he was on top of the game.

It is, perhaps, fortunate for the Scratchman that they don't see his second shot, a rather snatchy little jerk, so that he plays his third from under a tree and subsequently just manages to shovel in a curly 4-footer for a half in five, but by this time they're too busy with troubles of their own. And in any case the Scratchman, if he's up to his work, greets the snatchy little jerk with a cry of such genuine amusement and surprise that even his partner Willy, who was confidently anticipating a three, is moved to look upon it in the same light—i.e. a laughable aberration, solely due to Pernod and tiny actresses, and one which will certainly not occur again. When it does occur, again and again, the Scratchman's pantomime of bewildered astonishment is so amusingly played that Willy almost comes to the conclusion that he was doing it on purpose, even after they've been beaten four and three—despite some extraordinarily gallant putting, with a lot of green-sweeping and line assessing, by the Scratchman

HOW TO BECOME A SCRATCH GOLFER

none of which actually finished in the hole. Even their opponents feel they were pretty lucky to win and can't make out, indeed, exactly how they did, specially by such a large margin.

They have been dazzled by Scratchman's Aura.

Let us—before we, too, are blinded—set down the principles of this vital factor in the game.

PRINCIPLES OF SCRATCHMAN'S AURA

(1) An absolute ban on all clothing specifically designed for golf, with particular reference to zippered jackets, rubberized shoes, felt caps and hairy jerseys. All these suggest an earnest, painstaking approach, the antithesis of Scratchman's Aura, which is alive with a swashbuckling quality, making it plain that he could play equally well in white tie and tails.

(2) Be deadly serious, however, about the shoes, which should outspike everything in the pro's shop. The shoes are the player's sole contact with the ground, and the source, therefore, of all power. Truly ferocious spikes indicate power unlimited.

(3) An absolutely leisured approach to the first tee, even at the risk of losing your place and generating a sense of grievance among the other members of the fourball which may poison the rest of the day. A real stinker played in an agitated hurry looks like a real stinker. A real stinker, played after long deliberation with the

caddy and a serious assessment of wind force, driver or brassie, line to the hole, etc. looks incomprehensible.

(4) No trolleys, please, over the age of twenty-one. You can't discuss the next shot with a trolley. A slashing 3-iron into the teeth of the wind, finishing a yard from the stick, looks as if you've done it on purpose, if it follows a low-voiced conference with a caddy. Without the conference and the caddy it looks like the fluke which it is.

(5) Never call the caddy "Caddy", but use the nickname by which he is known only to other caddies who work with professionals on the tournament circuit. Drop it, without explanation, to handicap players who've never heard of him. Over-tip him sickeningly and in private at the end of the round, so that his eagerness for your patronage will be ascribed to the brillance of your game.

(6) Never complain about the partner you get stuck with. It suggests anxiety about the result, which will probably be exactly the same anyway.

(7) Always confess, using a broad comedy routine, to a crippling hangover, in case you get an opening blow which finishes behind the ladies' teebox. Indicate, clearly, that the hangover comes not from beer swilling in the golf-club bar, in which handicap men might engage, and probably have, but from an evening out with Ava Gardner, at the very least, so that even your

partner will think it reasonable for you to start with three sixes and a seven.

(8) Get a crippling hangover, if you've never had one, and make a careful note of the tottering, pole-axed symptoms, so that you'll be able to play them up to the hilt on return performances.

(9) Never, ever, have a practice swing. You've got to be very good indeed before a practice swing looks like the harbinger of 270 yards straight down the middle. A practice swing often hits the ground or someone else's trolley. Even if it doesn't it will only represent a panic-stricken attempt—obvious to everyone—to try to assess what's likely to happen when and if a golf-ball intrudes itself into the carpet-beating flog which this morning appears to represent your normal method of striking.

(10) Instantly drop all larking about, jokes and hangover mimes when your turn comes to play. It suggests a Palmer-like concentration which may not be borne out by the results, but at least gives you the opportunity to look genuinely astonished when your tee-shot trickles along the ground.

(11) When your tee-shot trickles along the ground reveal first of all astonishment and then honest amusement, in which all present should be freely invited to join. When you top the next one, leaving it still in the rough, return to the hangover mime.

(12) If you do get a good one, instantly start to talk

about something else or, preferably, elaborate the theme you were on when the others were playing theirs. This shows that 250 yards down the middle is routine, and not a profound surprise.

It should be noted here that the creation of Scratchman's Aura has nothing whatever to do with Gamesmanship.

Gamesmanship is an introverted defence mechanism fundamentally concerned with winning, an ambition which is actually despised by the true Scratchman who hasn't won a match in years because his handicap really ought to be eleven.

The Gamesman who, in action, often resembles an elderly charlady beating a carpet in a gale of wind, seeks to depress his opponents below his own level of incompetence by playing upon their neuroses, because only victory can provide an assuagement for his own.

The Scratchman, on the other hand, cares nothing for victory. He accepts it cheerfully, if it comes without a struggle. It would never occur to him, however, to try to bring victory about by putting his opponents off. Their game is of absolutely no concern to him. All that he asks, while paying out yet more folding money in the bar, is that they should believe him to be infinitely better than they are and that he would certainly have been round in 69 gross with a little better luck.

The Scratchman often does, in fact, win matches by the sheer bravura of his performance.

Inexperienced players, dazzled by the radiance, often

HOW TO BECOME A SCRATCH GOLFER

find it difficult to spot him, and go down without a struggle five-and-four. It is only afterwards, in the bar, when the Scratchman is talking modestly about being "a couple over fours", that if they take the trouble to add it up they find he was actually round in 83, though it *looked* as if it was a great deal less.

There are two methods of piercing this shining armour.

(1) Ask the Scratchman to hole short putts on the first four greens. If he's a genuine Scratchman he'll hit the back of the hole with all four of them, taking extreme pains with each. If he's one of the flash boys he'll miss at least two and, despite his merry, incredulous laughter, you'll know him for what he is.

(2) Have a little chat with his caddy, heaping excessive praise on the fluency of Sir's swing. The caddy, who carried Joe Carr's bag in the Amateur of '52 and therefore has his own reputation to consider, will quickly put you straight.

Quite a number of handicap players, wearing zippered jackets and green berets, with their trousers tucked into the ends of their socks, go out of their way, even to the extent of incurring a social rebuff, to invite the flash Scratchman to demean himself by joining in their rough fourball.

They know it will pay for their lunch.

7

PRACTICE LOSES THE LOT

In the ordinary golf club where, perhaps, about a hundred members might play regularly, three of them are figures of fun.

They are the ones—the proportion is usually about 3%—who use the practice ground for the purpose of improving their game.

The other 97 wouldn't dream of going near it. Like 97% of all golfers everywhere they believe that next time out, for reasons to be analysed later in the bar, they will play the game of their lives. It will just come, out of the blue, and stay with them for ever. They feel that there is no point in practising, seeing that this miraculous improvement is guaranteed by Fate.

There may be something to be said for them, in view of the fact that the 3% who do practise, practise a game which they are exceedingly unlikely to play on the course.

I recall a time—it was Hogan's *Power Golf* that did it to me again—when I resolved to rebuild my game from the ground up with a rigorous course of practice in the garden. A hundred shots before breakfast, lunch, tea and dinner—that sort of thing.

HOW TO BECOME A SCRATCH GOLFER

I bought a practice net, rigged between two poles supported by guy ropes, and set it up in such a way that a loose one would fly harmlessly into a neighbouring field. I then cut out from *Power Golf* the series of photographs

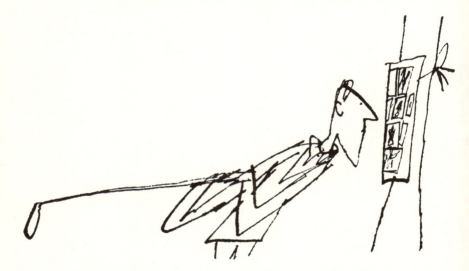

depicting Hogan at work with his driver and pasted them, in sequence, on a sheet of cardboard. This meant buying two copies of *Power Golf*, to get the photographs on the back of the preceding page, but it was plain the expense was going to be worth it.

I started to practise, then, with the series of photographs tacked to a neighbouring tree.

Power golf took over immediately. The first shot with the driver was so powerful that it went clean through the netting and disappeared into the field, leaving a large hole behind it. The netting, as far as I could make out, must

have been intended for the reception of tiny iron shots played by very young girls, so I dug some disused underfelt out of the beams of the garage and draped that over the netting, as an additional fortification. The weight pulled the guy ropes out of the ground and the whole thing fell down. The miserable little pegs provided by the manufacturers were clearly inadequate. I substituted some old iron bars, hammered them a couple of feet down into the lawn and set up the whole fortified apparatus all over again. It now looked sufficiently robust to defy a tank.

The next shot with the driver missed it altogether. In the Hogan style I had my chin well cocked and the head right down at the moment of impact, so that I never saw where it went. After waiting for what felt like an hour for the crash of glass or a cry of pain I guessed that the ball had found some harmless destination. Rather than have the same period of anxiety again I moved much closer to the net for the next one and was rewarded by a solid thunk as the ball hit the under-felt. The first one had probably passed right over the top of it.

A hundred shots later I found that the lawn had taken a lot of punishment, particularly from the push with the inside of the right foot at the moment of impact, but there was no doubt at all that extra power was here. Holes were beginning to appear in the under-felt, even after I'd hung a bedspread over it to take the initial shock.

It was, as may be imagined, with high expectation that I took this new swing on to the golf course the following Saturday morning, going so far as to tell my caddy that I was "doing it the Hogan way now".

Big, wide arc going back, dragging the hands down to initiate the down swing, hips going round to face the hole and a pistol-like crack as the club-face met the ball. Missing the familiar thunk as it hit the under-felt, I looked up to see where the drive had gone and could find no trace of it in the surrounding scenery.

I looked at my caddy, in search of a clue, and saw his

mouth open. He was staring, in astonishment, in the direction of cover point. Following his eyeline, at about 45° to the intended line of flight, I saw the ball passing quail-high, having carried more than 200 yards, over a distant hedge and out of bounds.

This, with the rigid Hogan left arm, turned out to have been the shot I'd been practising with such devotion all week, deprived by the nearness of the netting, however, from seeing its ultimate development. It was another week before I was able to bend one back on to the course again.

Practice with a net, therefore, should be attempted only by players so expert that they can tell, purely by feel, where the shot has gone, and if there are any of those around I wouldn't mind meeting them.

The practice ground is a wiser investment for the ordinary player. At least here he can see the result, but he's going to need a caddy to pick them up.

Without a caddy practice is likely to be brought to a premature end through lack of ammunition, as we shall see in:

CASE HISTORY NUMBER FIVE

Jack is a large and powerfully built young man who has been playing golf for two years, and sees it as the only human activity of any worth.

He is so keen, indeed, that he refuses to join in a jolly Sunday morning fourball, in favour of what he calls "a work-out" on the practice ground.

He's been reading too many American golf books.

What Americans mean by "a work-out" is a flexing of

their superbly trained muscles in the reproduction of the same shot over and over again.

What Jack means by "a work-out", though he doesn't know it, is a series of experiments, using half a dozen different styles, in an attempt to hit six successive shots comparatively straight.

It's a blustery morning, with the wind blowing across the practice ground and the morning sun still rather low at the eastern end.

Jack starts off with the sun behind him, tipping about a dozen balls out of the bag and taking a 4-iron.

He's never quite sure how far a 4-iron is going to go, so he plays a nice easy one in the general direction of the other end of the practice ground. The result, inconceivably, is a socket. The ball disappears almost at right angles into the undergrowth bordering the practice ground about thirty yards away.

Jack looks round cautiously to see if he has been observed. Several of his fellow members—the lazy incompetents who can never be bothered to practise though God knows they need it—have jeered at his enthusiasm before now.

Four of them, naturally enough, have been privileged to see Jack's opening shot from half-way down the first fairway. They call out encouraging advice. "No need to practise that one, Jack, you've got it made." And so on. They stand there, with four caddies, making an audience of eight, to watch his next one.

Determined to avoid another socket, and jokes which will take a week to die, Jack keeps his head right down on this one and hits the ball a good, firm blow with his right hand. It feels all right, but it's disappeared by the time he looks up to follow its flight. The chorus of derision from the audience gives him no clue to its direction. Jack makes a mental note to look for it in the short rough on the left.

Some minutes later, at the other end of the practice ground, Jack wishes he'd counted his total of balls more carefully. He's nearly sure he'd started with about twelve, but now there seem to be only eight left. He remembers the one he socketed into the bushes. That makes nine. Jack decides the others will probably turn up, and hits three shots back into the sun. He sees nothing of any of them, but they didn't feel too bad, so he knocks up the other five.

At the other end of the practice ground there is no sign of any golf balls at all. All eight practice shots have vanished without a trace and the practice ground is nearly a hundred yards wide.

After a long search Jack finds the first one—the one he knocked into the bushes—and three more at widely spaced intervals in the rough on either side.

If he has any sense, having lost eight balls in ten minutes, he will now withdraw to the putting green in front of the clubhouse where, even if it doesn't do his putting any good, another half hour's practice will leave him with the same amount of ammunition as he started with.

This is the only benefit that can come to someone who practises by himself.

Scientific practice—which will probably revolutionize one's whole game—can be enjoyed only with the help of a caddy to pick up the spray of stuff which tends to emerge.

The caddy, however, must be prepared to cover considerable distances at a trot and should therefore be under fifteen years of age.

Older caddies actually hinder practice.

On one occasion, sharpening up for the Halford Hewitt at Deal, I got one who must have been approaching seventy, as a result of negotiations with the caddy master, which have taken the same form for years.

"Good morning, friend. Got a good, strong horse for me with an eye like an eagle?"

"I've had the blanket on him all night. He's full of bran mash and rarin' to go. Give us your harness and we'll strap it on."

On this occasion, after we'd strapped the harness on to the seventy year old horse, I told him we'd go down to the practice ground "for a bit of a loosen up", as we weren't off for another hour.

The old man looked at me with loathing, an attention he'd already paid to my bag of clubs. He humped them on to his shoulder, raised his red-rimmed eyes to the sky and stumped off to the practice ground, followed at a discreet distance by myself.

When we arrived it was to find a number of the stars of the tournament, including several Blues, already rifling shots far into the distance. I chose an empty space well away from them.

My caddy lowered the bag to the ground and started, with a patent machine, to roll himself a very thin and shaggy cigarette.

"Perhaps," I said, "you'd like to get out there and pick up a few shots—?"

He completed his manufacture of the cigarette, lit it, put his hands in the pockets of his voluminous overcoat and set off.

About a hundred yards away he turned and stood looking at me mournfully, the hands still in his overcoat pockets.

I made various signs indicating that I wanted him to go farther away. After a long time he shrugged hopelessly, turned on his fallen arches and retreated about another fifty yards.

I took out the driver and hit a beauty, well over his head.

He made no movement of any kind. It was clear he hadn't seen it at all.

I did a lot more waving, trying to drive him still farther back. After nearly a minute he seemed to get my meaning and plodded off again, nearly out of sight against the ditch bordering the far field.

The second shot was a lot less effective than the first—a quick hook which nearly decapitated one of the Blues' caddies and disappeared into the field on the left.

My eagle eyed horse didn't see that one either.

Of the next dozen shots five of them finished in the field, two were topped and the remainder were pushed miles out to the right. The five in the field were wisely ignored by my helper who was, however, good enough to pick up the others. It took him a long time as they weren't exactly together. In mid-trek across the practice ground he paused at one moment to confer with his colleague, who scarcely had to move at all to pick up his master's contribution. I judged he was telling him that you get all sorts in the Halford Hewitt.

When he returned to me, with what remained of our supplies, he put them straight back in the bag, picked it up and stumped off to the first tee. Though we still had another half hour to go it was clear that our loosening-up process was over.

Practice, then, to be perfect needs an overcast day, a fleet-footed young retriever and, I should say, the attendance of at least one assistant professional to keep the player up to scratch—or as close to it as he is ever likely to get.

I've never been really devoted to it myself, not since

the morning Henry Longhurst caught me at it at Lytham St. Annes.

He watched me play half-a-dozen not absolutely immaculate mid-irons. Then he spoke.

"It will take you," he said, "at least seventy-nine shots to get round. If I were you I wouldn't waste any of them here. You're liable to run out of steam."

8

MUZZLE THE RULES—THEY BITE!

Of all the little things that serve to enrage players of the genial and friendly game of golf none does so with greater certainty than the behaviour of the staggeringly incompetent egomaniacs playing in the match ahead.

As we stand here, miming exasperation and incredulity on the fifteenth tee, having been held up by them since the third, there seems to us to be no limit to the length of time it could take them to complete this perfectly simple hole.

Calmly and objectively speaking, it is impossible to make an analysis of what they think they're doing.

They're doing it now, crouched in the long grass miles away out in the rough on the right, apparently effecting running repairs to one of their trolleys, though they could equally easily be playing cards.

On the face of it, the solution would appear to be simple. Merely drive off, and play through. Yet we know better. We know that the moment we start our back swing they will be warned of it by some telepathic mechanism. They will spring from their nests in the rough like snipe, rush into the middle of the fairway and start up another of the conversations which enliven their game.

These little chats seemed to be built upon two basic enquiries. They take place out of earshot, about 150 yards away, but we can tell what's going on by the gestures.

The basic enquiries are:

"Is that your ball—or mine?"

"Is it my turn to play—or yours?"

They live, these two men, in a fog of incomprehension. After they hit it, they don't know where it's gone. When they find it five minutes later in the rough on the right, having searched every inch of the rough on the left, they think it's the other man's ball. When, after another little chat, they find that it is, indeed, their own, they take out a 5-iron to extricate it, have two practice swings with the 5-iron and then put it back in the bag, in favour of a 4-wood. Then they hit it three yards into deeper undergrowth than it was in before.

But this business moves like lightning in comparison

with their performance on the greens. It takes them a long time to reach the green from the tee but when they get there they really settle to their work.

They advance upon the flagstick from opposite directions, and both grasp it at the same time. They pass it backwards and forwards. It looks like Morris dancing. One of them finally accepts the stick and lays it down on the green.

The other settles to play his approach putt and finds that the stick is now lying across his line, so he advances to pick it up. The other one, at the same moment, decides to do likewise, so they pass it backwards and forwards from hand to hand all over again. Then they put the stick well out of the way and take three putts each. Both the first two putts are followed by statuesque poses, held for nearly a minute, indicating astonishment that the ball has not dropped. Then they pick up the stick and pass it from hand to hand until one of them manages to insert it into the hole.

At this moment the players waiting behind might be entitled to suppose that the proceedings on this green, at least, had reached a terminal point, but it is not so.

Both wreckers have left their trolleys on the front edge of the green. They walk back to them, very slowly, discussing how many shots each thinks the other has played, with the intention of noting it down on a scorecard.

It is impossible to guess why they want to do this. They are not playing in the medal, because that was last Saturday. They are certainly not marking cards to put them in for handicap adjustment because neither of them has ever bothered with this technicality, nor are they ever likely to do so, seeing that both their handicaps stand at an absolutely irreducible maximum of twenty-four.

They mark down their scores, looking over one another's shoulders to watch the miracle of writing. Then they seize their trolleys and walk off to the next tee, but one of them has still got another ace to play. He starts off round the righthand side of the green and suddenly remembers—he's been playing the course for twenty years—that it's a bit hilly for a trolley that way so he turns about, walks all the way back again, makes a stately promenade right across the front of the green and rejoins his mate on the left.

We, waiting to play our second shots 200 yards away, hit both of them two feet.

Fortunately, redress against this sort of thing is provided by the Rules of Golf.

In Section I, under the heading of ETIQUETTE, the following Rule appears:

"If a match fails to keep its place on the course and loses more than one clear hole on the players in front, it should allow the match following it to pass."

That, one would imagine, should make matters clear enough, but of course it doesn't. Like all the Rules of Golf this one is open to individual interpretation, a process which can lead to threats of violence if not to the actual exchange of blows.

I remember once playing in a match behind a ponderous American fourball at Temple, outside Maidenhead, where the incumbent, Henry Cotton, has seen fit to provide two electric buggies.

One of these buggies was being used by a powerfully

constructed U.S.A.F. Major who looked as if he had the strength not only to walk but to run right round the course without stopping. He chose, however, to sit in the buggy, travelling along very slowly in the wake of his companions who, like all Americans, were playing at funereal speed.

Going up the hill from the fifteenth tee the Major's buggy finally ground to a halt, having been promising to do so for some time. He sat in it, hunched and cursing. Heavy rain was falling. By the way he'd been playing I guessed he was probably about 150 dollars down to his friends.

Suddenly, it seemed a good time to remind him that he'd already lost at least two holes on the match ahead.

"Fore!" I called, penetratingly.

He didn't move for a moment or two. It was as though he'd been shot. Then he got out of the buggy, very slowly, and turned to identify the source of the warning. He was wearing a thing like a baseball cap, and smoking a large, damp cigar.

My companions withdrew quietly from the tee, leaving me standing there alone.

The Major pushed up the peak of his baseball cap and came walking back towards me at a steady pace. He stopped, less than a foot away, and removed his cigar.

"One more yip out of you, Mac," he said, "and I'll bust you right in the snoot."

He paused, measuring me, then added, "Check?"

I nodded curtly, short of a more adroit riposte.

The Major re-inserted his cigar, tramped back to his buggy, pushed it over the crest of the hill and disappeared from view. At my request we waited until they were on the next tee before driving off from our own.

Excluding the nine Rules of Etiquette and in Section II the thirty-four "Definitions", there are forty-one Rules of Play, nearly all of which have about half-a-dozen sub-sections, and with the possible exception of Rule I—"The Game of Golf consists in playing a ball from the teeing ground into the hole by successive strokes in accordance with the Rules"—all of them are lively provokers of strife.

For this reason the expert player prefers to leave them strictly alone, an abstinence assisted by his almost total ignorance of their content.

Up till January 1st, 1960, a few class men could give you a rough quote of some of the better known ones, but then the Royal and Ancient amended them and pretty well everyone gave up.

Golf, in fact, is the only game in the world in which a precise knowledge of the rules can earn one a reputation for bad sportsmanship.

Novices coming into the game for the first time should be chary of reading them, and even more so of attempting to put them into practice, if the round is to be completed in under three hours. The next Case History illustrates the point.

CASE HISTORY NUMBER SIX

Noel L— played the violin in a Dublin orchestra, but took over the baton at rehearsals when the conductor went out for a cup of tea or, more probably—I knew him, too—a pint of stout.

I can't imagine, in view of Noel's interests, how our social paths ever crossed but when they did the meeting left me committed to playing a round of golf with him, a subject which had cropped up via the unlikely forcing ground of a discussion about the fingering of "The Flight of the Bumblebee", a piece apparently containing so many semi-quavers that it left even hardened violinists with the equivalent of writer's cramp. But not, by his own testimony, Noel, the demon fiddler. He, it seemed, kept his fingering up to the output, in speed and precision, of a pneumatic drill by playing golf. "The club," he said—and I'd never heard the principles of the Vardon Grip enunciated by a more improbable source—"is entwined in the fingers. Mine are like whipcord."

They looked like spaghetti but I was prepared, in view of his undoubted mastery of the Bumblebee selection, to believe him. I even hoped I might learn something from watching his whipcord finger action, as I was persistently striking the ground behind the ball at this time, all the power seeming to come from the lower back.

When we arrived, the following morning, on the first tee it was occupied by two solid bookmakers and a distinguished Irish amateur, all three of whom were well known to play for sums of money so large that the distinguished amateur scarcely ever felt compelled to go to his office.

The two bookmakers had already driven off. Their tee-shots lay almost side by side, a long way down the middle of the fairway. They were useful players but not, as the

HOW TO BECOME A SCRATCH GOLFER

distinguished amateur had discovered to his satisfaction, quite useful enough.

"Hello, there," he said to me, "do you want to play through?" This was purely a formality as he'd seen me play before and had even given me some advice about hooking which I'd been unable to put into practice.

I was about, as he expected, to deny any such ambition

when Noel spoke. "Thanks," he said. "That's very good of you. Thanks very much indeed."

He was wearing, I want to point out, white tennis shoes, grey flannels and an open-necked cricket shirt turned neatly down over the collar of a light-brown sports jacket.

I demurred. I told them to carry on, that we were in no hurry. It was a suspicion that had entered my mind in the locker room, when I saw the demon fiddler putting on his tennis shoes.

But Noel was already teeing up his ball or, rather, trying to balance it on a plastic tee in the shape of a three-legged milking stool attached to a length of red wool which terminated in a large red bobble of the same material.

"Just a minute," I said, "let them carry on. We'll only hold them up."

"I'm afraid we can't do that," said Noel crisply. "Twosomes have priority over threesomes, you see. It's in the rules."

I don't think any of us had heard the word "twosome" used on a golf course before. The bookmakers and the distinguished amateur stood down. They had the look of men who found it difficult to believe a sequence of events that was taking place before their very eyes.

They believed what they were seeing even less after Noel had played his opening blow. He was very short indeed going back, the club-head rising no higher than his knee. To generate power, therefore, he slid his right tennis shoe forward at the moment of impact, crossed it over the left one and then, just as we presumed he'd finished his stroke, he added on a long, jerky follow-through to conclude the performance, incredibly, with his face framed between his arms, the club held vertically above his head and the plastic milking-stool, with its red wool and bobble, wound several times around the shaft. The ball rolled gently sideways perhaps fifteen feet, and finished underneath some wire netting protecting the other half of the tee.

He disentangled himself, and the plastic milking stool, and suddenly showed concern. "Oh, dear," he said, "perhaps I ought to have that again. I mean, wasn't it your honour? Lowest handicap plays first."

I said it didn't matter.

Noel nodded. "Actually," he said, "it is just a convention. In Rule Twelve, sub-section one, it says that in the absence of a draw, the option of taking the honour shall be decided by lot."

Out of the corner of my eye I saw the bookmakers and the distinguished amateur exchange surprised looks. It was news to them, too, by the look of it.

"Perhaps," said Noel, "you'd like to toss for the honour, so we can start properly?"

"Why don't you do that?" said one of the bookmakers. "It's only eleven o'clock in the morning. We've got all day."

Noel seemed actually to be searching in his pockets for a coin.

To speed our departure from the tee I took a very quick swish at mine, coming down from the top like an express lift. The ball rose perhaps thirty feet in the air and plugged itself in the middle of the fairway about fifty yards away.

"Shot," said Noel, with genuine appreciation. He

picked up his small, drainpipe bag by the strap—it was made of canvas in what looked like the Royal Stuart tartan—and, trailing it behind him, walked over to his own ball.

"Look," I said to the distinguished amateur, "you'd really better carry on. We're just messing about—"

But he was staring over my shoulder. We were, indeed, messing about. Noel was already playing his second or, rather, his second, third, fourth and fifth, a series of delicate little taps on top of the wire netting, aimed at getting his ball back into play. He paused before the sixth stroke to remark, "Bad place," and then returned to his work.

I hurried over to him. "Pick it out, you ass. That's ground under repair."

He looked surprised. "What's ground under repair?"

"I thought you knew the rules."

"Only some of them," replied Noel courteously. "I haven't been playing long."

In the end I lifted up the netting and he scooped the ball out with an iron. He produced his plastic milking-stool again, teed the ball and struck it diagonally across the course into a patch of brambles on the left. "That's better," said Noel.

I was about to tell him that he wasn't allowed to tee his ball on the fairway, but thought better of it. At any moment the bookmakers and the distinguished amateur might recover from their surprise, and become impatient. I walked up to my ball—it was more than half buried in the mud—and was about to pick it out when Noel said, "That's not ground under repair, you know."

"Go away," I said. "It's a local rule."

"That's not fair," said Noel belligerently. "You're just making it up."

Without looking at them, I could tell that the players behind must have just about reached breaking point.

"All right," I said. I dug the ball out of the mud and put it in my pocket. "I'll give you the hole."

"That's the fairest thing," Noel agreed. "I'll just finish it off then," he said, "for practice."

He found it in an unplayable lie in the brambles or, at least, it would have been unplayable to anyone else. Noel, however, reached in one-handed with his iron, tongue protruding in deep concentration, and scooped it out towards him, playing—if they were countable at all—perhaps twelve shots. Then he teed it up again on his milking stool and by a miracle hit one straight. "It's the strength in the fingers that does it," he said, and marched off after it.

When I caught up with him I said, "You're not allowed to tee up your ball on the fairway. You can only use a tee to tee it up on the tee." My mind was giving way with the need to explain it at all.

"Oh," said Noel, interested. "I never knew that." He stopped. "I'd better go back and play another one," he said, "properly."

At this moment the distinguished amateur decided to take matters into his own hands. He let go with a shot that passed over our heads with the sound and speed of a bullet.

I was unprepared for Noel's reaction. He threw down his bag, turned to face the oncoming match, and roared "Fore!" It was the first time I'd ever heard the cry in, as it were, reverse.

They walked through us in silence, three deeply shocked and angry men.

Noel had the final word. "Bad sports!" he shouted after them.

It took us perhaps three hours to complete the rest of the round, locked in altercation about the Rules of Golf. I became inured in the end to Noel's furtive attempts to tee up his ball in the rough when I wasn't looking, but continued to object to his habit of tapping it backwards and forwards with his putter, while it was still in motion, until it gave up the struggle and fell into the hole.

"We'd have had a much better match," Noel said in the bar afterwards, "if you hadn't been so finicky about the rules."

Fundamentally, he was right.

9

NOW NO GOOD, SAME LIKE YOU

Sooner or later, as the player advances along the narrow fairways leading to Scratchdom, he will probably find himself assisting professional golfers to win serious money in pro-amateur tournaments, the most socially glittering of which is the Bowmaker Tournament at Sunningdale.

Here, the professional plays 36 holes medal, so that he puts in three scores—one off his own bat, one his best ball with Amateur A, and one his best ball with Amateur B.

It often takes Amateurs A and B several hours of patient listening and questioning to understand the system, but an example usually makes all clear.

If the pro takes five at the first, which he usually does, and Amateurs A and B take four and six respectively, the three cards will read:

Pro: 5.
Pro plus A: 4.
Pro plus B: 5.

From this it will be seen that while the amateur can improve the pro's score, he cannot make it any worse, a comfort to the amateur when quick hooking breaks out, if not to the pro.

HOW TO BECOME A SCRATCH GOLFER

Last year at Sunningdale, on his own card, the pro stood to win £350, and with one of the other amateurs, £250, so that the pro has a sympathetic interest in his partner's progress. One year, playing with Ugo Grappasoni, from the Villa d'Este, I discovered how sympathetic this interest could be.

We played the first nine holes in complete silence owing, as I thought, to Ugo's failure to come to grips with the English language. I wanted to speak to him, as I wasn't playing very well. When I got one off the tee that finished on the fairway I put the next one into the woods. When I got one off the tee that finished in the woods I picked it up.

Ugo watched these enervating activities with a cold black eye that put me in mind of vendettas and the Mafia's revenge.

Held up briefly on the ninth, I decided to take a chance on speech. I asked him if, perhaps, I was doing something fractionally wrong. The right hand creeping a shade too far underneath? A minute fault in the stance—the ball, perhaps, half an inch too far back—?

Ugo made his first and last observation of the day. "Isa ponch, ponch," he said. "Isa noh swing. Isa a whole t'ing isa noh good."

That's the kind of discovery the budding Scratchman is liable to make when he moves up into the big time. Isa whole t'ing isa noh good. And the professionals do not hesitate to tell him so, with £250 slipping out of their hands into the bushes.

I played a year later with Leopoldo Ruiz, the Thin Crust of Bread from the Argentine, whom I have already mentioned.

In the first round Leopoldo, taking a 2-iron off the tee and hitting all of them 270-yards, notched a spirited 65, unassisted in any way whatever by myself.

In the second round, however, he got a bad kick with his pitch to the seventh and found an unplayable lie in a small bush at the back of the green. He prowled round it for some time with cries of, "Carrramba!" and "Mamma mia!", had a hack at it, knocked it into the deep bunker on the left and finished with a seven. Things began to go wrong from then on until, after failing to get anything like a three at the short fifteenth, Leopoldo abandoned hope. He turned to me with charming Latin-American courtesy. "Now," he growled, "I play no blahdy good, same like you."

Last year I played with colourful Max Faulkner, who turned up for the first round in three shades of primrose, which included his shoes.

The first tee at Sunningdale is always something of an ordeal in this Bowmaker Tournament. It's too close to the club-house and the putting green, so that there is liable to be an audience of several hundred people, including pro's trying to hole six foot putts.

Furthermore, when your turn comes to play, your name is announced by the starter, coupled with the reason why you were invited to play at all. This is usually based upon some sort of notoriety in the fields of stage, screen, journalism or sport.

Max drove first, slashing one 300-yards down the middle, apparently unencumbered by the three shades of primrose, and then the starter called out, "Patrick Campbell—the well-known humorist."

Those who were watching must have doubted the description. A friend of mine said afterwards, "I thought you were going to cry."

Off the first tee at Sunningdale there are two alternatives, disregarding the straight shot down the middle which, I find, comes once every five years in the Bowmaker.

You can slash it over the trees on the right on to the road, or hook it on to the eighteenth fairway, up which Archbishop Arthur d'Arcy Locke is probably marching at this moment, attended by several hundred disciples.

I chose the trees and taking the club back well outside the line, tried to slice the maker's name off the ball. It turned out to be very nearly a good one, going a long way but drifting at the last moment into a large clump of brambles.

As we stepped off the tee I saw colourful Max looking at me with some curiosity. Then he spoke. "How long have you been hitting 'em like that, mate?"

Shocked, I could think of no explanatory rejoinder.

"Your nut," said Max, "is shifting three feet on the back swing. Keep it steady, for God's sake."

Six holes later I managed to hit one straight. "There you are, you see, mate," said Max, "there's nothing to it at all." He was really happy to see another soul saved from the burning.

It is, of course, this opening blow off the first tee, as we've already demonstrated, that separates the sheep from the goats, and the division has never been more sharply marked than it was at Rosses Point, in a West of Ireland Championship, round about 1935.

In those days—the situation remains unchanged—I always tried to hit them out of sight with the driver and was therefore a constant victim of what big hitters call pre-ignition—that one that goes off before the player is ready for it.

On this occasion I wasn't really ready for anything, having been called once again from the poker table in the club-house at 9.5 a.m., being due to start at 9 o'clock. Full, however, of spirit, I decided upon a really big one off the first tee to get the day off to a flying, if belated, start.

At the top of the swing I suddenly discovered that the really big one had turned into a giant—that was, an enormously wide arc and a pivot so full that the left shoulder felt as if it had got under the right ear. These preliminaries had raised my hands so high in the air that I could think, in the brief time at my disposal, of no method of getting them down and into the neighbourhood of the ball except by a convulsive ducking of the knees—an instinctive gesture, really, aimed at reducing the dizzy and unnatural height of the whole structure.

Because of the speed it was difficult for me to follow the events that happened next, but it seemed that the clubhead, whistling down from the height of ten feet, struck the ground like a bomb, bounced forward and after completing a full circle round my neck finished up pointing sole-foremost at the distant hole.

In view of the speed of the swing and the fact that it contained at least three unrelated parts, I'd little hope that the ball, of which I'd seen nothing after starting the back swing, had gone very far or very straight, but even so I was unprepared for the actuality. It was revealed to me by my opponent, a dog trainer of genial disposition called Mick. He was staring at the secretary's tent on the right of the tee.

"Jaysus," called Mick joyfully, "yez have him killed!"

"He" turned out to be the secretary in person. As we entered the tent, at a run, we found him sitting at a small card table, frozen into immobility, his pencil still poised over the draw-sheet on which he'd been working when my tee-shot came in through the open doorway, to strike the canvas behind his head with such a loud report that he thought—as he was able to tell us when he regained the power of speech—that "some eejit took a belt at me with a stick outside."

In the end, after a discussion about the meaning of unnatural hazards and temporary structures, we resolved an absurd situation by deeming my ball unplayable—it was lying in a corner of the tent behind a wastepaper basket—and I dropped out, subsequently losing the hole to a six.

Mick commiserated with me as we walked to the next tee. "It was catchin' the ground that done you," he said seriously. "If you'd 'a got her fair and square she'd 'a been clean through th'ole tent and out the other side."

He was right. The only secret of big hitting is to get her fair and square with all you've got.

Unfortunately, to achieve this combination of perfections, or Amateur's Fluke, you've got to have something like a real golf swing, coupled with considerable physical strength. Mere height is not so important.

I remember once galloping round the corner of the clubhouse at the Berkshire carrying a heavy bag of clubs and running full tilt into Norman von Nida who, with his back turned to me, was conversing with some friends. Despite the fact that Norman is about 5 ft. 6 in., it was like hitting a tree. He turned to look at me as I lay on the ground.

"Watch it, cobber," he said, and resumed the critical remarks he was making about the quality of the greens. It was easy to feel where his length came from.

There's a great deal of pleasure in playing with professionals, if you can keep the stakes down, or pick the winner.

They are, for the most part, exceedingly genial men devoted to the sensation of striking a golf ball, and prepared to tell anyone in the bar afterwards exactly how they played every one of the 68 shots it took them to get round, though they are inclined to be more reticent if it turns out to be 79.

Playing with professionals puts a polish on the amateur's game which often dazzles him. It has the same effect upon the members of his regular Sunday morning fourball, when he returns to them, although they know that everything will be back to normal next week. But however high the polish may be, unless he has a natural talent for it, one department of the amateur's game is liable to remain permanently dingy.

Putting.

The simple act of rolling the ball into the hole over distances as short as two feet.

It would seem to be impossible to miss at this range, in view of the fact that the hole is approximately twice the width of the ball.

Let us see how easily it can be done.

10

CONE BALLS AND SHRINKAGE

Of all the tools in the golfer's sack none is as personal to him as his putter.

Bobby Jones, when he won the Grand Slam—the British Open and Amateur and the American Open and Amateur—in the same year, did it with the help of a weapon called Calamity Jane, a hickory shafted stick with three narrow bands of whipping which might have made all the difference to Bobby Jones but subsequently did little for anyone else when Calamity Jane was mass-produced.

Max Faulkner has been the owner of—I think he told me—seventy-two putters in his time. The last time I played with him he was using a tool with a shaft made of driftwood and a rusted head on the back of which was stamped the date 1884.

Some people have putters with square heads and play it between their legs like a croquet mallet.

Some elderly gentlemen roll them in from all over the place with horrible things with aluminium heads and a style that obviously shouldn't work, but does, every single time.

American women have putters made of white marble with a floral motif.

American professionals hardly ever miss from 8-feet with centre-shafted putters.

Wall Street Financiers play with putters made of gold.

Some people buy a new putter every month and with it continue to knock the ball harmlessly past the left-hand side of the hole, apart from the very first one which goes in, compelling them to buy yet another new putter, to achieve the same effect.

My father played for years with a putter with a brass head four inches long and a crack in the shaft, so that sometimes it produced an audible clonk when he hit the ball. "When you get the clonk," he used to say, "you're all right," despite persistent evidence to the contrary.

When he gave it to me I couldn't hole one from 18-inches with it, even when I did get the clonk.

The next putter I owned was a miracle of design with a beautifully smooth ebony head and a steel shaft precision-bent to get the hands right over the ball. It flew to pieces one day when I missed yet again from two-feet and in a tempest of rage tried to hit the next one 200-yards.

After that I came upon a putter with a shaft bent backwards like the starting-handle of a car, so that at the address the hands were a couple of inches ahead of the club-face. It might have started a car.

Some years ago, however, I found my own true love, in Henry Cotton's shop at Temple.

What first attracted me to it was the length of the shaft. It was about the same as a 2-iron, towering above all the other putters in the rack.

I pounced on it and, being nearly 6 ft. 5 in., was for the first time in my life able to strike a putt without being bent double and subject to rushes of blood, lunch and other pressures.

It didn't go in, but the feeling of relaxation promised success in the future.

From Denis Scanlan in the shop I learnt that the putter had been designed by the Master himself, as a possible solution to his problems on the greens, and that it retailed at £3. 10s.

When the Master arrived in the Cadillac the following week-end I lost no time in striking a deal. "As I'm the only player for miles around that wouldn't get the handle of that putter stuck in his gullet," I said, "I'll take it off you for a quid."

Henry had a swish with it to see if he still liked it. He didn't. "If you want it," he said, "it will cost you five."

I protested that the putter was unsaleable to anyone else.

"That," said Henry, "is why it will cost you five."

In the end we settled for £3. 10s.

By hard bargaining of this kind the short game expert finds his own true love and, if he has any sense, remains faithful to her for the rest of his life.

It isn't the putter that strikes the ball. It's the player. But there are times when putters take on a life of their own.

Putters, drawn smoothly back in a line with the hole, are seen suddenly to be moving diagonally outwards. The movement is as irresistible as the tug of a divining rod.

The impulse that has drawn it out there is abruptly shut off, so that without warning the player once again finds himself in charge. But in charge of what?

The head of the putter is now six inches to the right of the correct line. The only thing to do is to pull it in in a semi-circle to get it behind the ball, shove it forward—and bad luck, old chap, I'm afraid that's the match.

It's beyond belief. The smallest, one-handed agitation of the club would have caused the ball to stagger forward two feet and drop into the hole, but here we've been struggling with divining rods and semi-circular pushes, practically a floral dance, to strike it so hard and so far off the line as to deprive us of any chance of holing the one back, should the need arise.

And yet, only yesterday, we were putting so well that we'd have been given this tiddler we've just missed, even by the rat who's just asked us to hole it, obviously inspired by the fact that we've failed to hole very similar ones on the last three greens.

When the floral dance breaks out on these short ones there is no limit to the delusions that can possess the player's mind. Like, for instance, Shrinking Ball.

Shrinking Ball develops from 6 feet inwards when we've got this one to save the match, and double the usual stakes, brought on by kümmel after lunch.

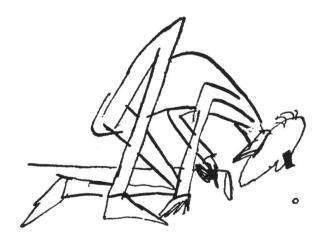

It looks quite ordinary while we survey the line, brushing away small obstructions and so on—all the familiar preparatory performance which is really aimed not at lining up the shot but at postponing the moment of hitting it. Before we hit it we've only played two. After we've hit it we'll be three, and will almost certainly have to hit it twice more before getting it into the hole. It feels more economical to prowl around it, on the green in two and playing to the strict par.

Sooner or later, however, something has to be done about it and it is at the moment we decide to do something about it that even the larger American ball appears to begin to decrease in size, and to start burrowing into the green.

When this happens the short game expert breaks off, picks up the ball and cleans it, in accordance with Rule 35 1-d: *A ball lying on the putting green may be lifted and cleaned without penalty and replaced on the spot from which it was lifted* . . . in the hope that the action of replacing it will plump it up a bit.

As we address it again the ball looks smaller and more deeply sunken than ever—and not only this but getting smaller and smaller and sinking more and more deeply so that we've got to strike it very quickly indeed before it disappears altogether below the surface. This is the one that shoots off six inches to the right of the hole, and leaves one's partner unable to speak. Subsequent, incredulous inspection of the putting surface reveals it to be dead level, unmarked even by the smallest depression.

Another cause of faulty work on the greens is Cone Ball, a disease that attacks strikers of long approach putts.

As we shape up to this one the ball appears to be cone-shaped, with the broad base resting on the ground. The longer we look at it the more convinced we become that the only way in which the ball can advance towards the hole is by skating along, without rotation, on its bottom. In order, therefore, to get the necessary length we're going to have to give it a good firm tap. This is the occasion upon which the club-head strikes the ground before the ball, so that the cone advances no more than three feet, leaving us with pretty much the same again.

I've always been convinced that Joe Carr, the great Irish amateur, was getting Cone Ball in the days when he

was putting with a 3-iron. Nothing else would have rendered him so impervious to the appeals of his supporters, all of whom would have substantial sums of currency at stake. "Not th'ole t'ree iron, Joe," they'd beg him. "Mosey it up with your putther—" But no man can mosey up a Cone Ball with his putter. Often he feels the only way to start it on its journey is with a wedge.

When things are not going too well on the greens the

ball and the club-head can, indeed, attain a phantasmagorical life of their own. I came across a particularly interesting case of this one year, playing in what is known to the cognoscenti as the Mixed Forplesdons at Worplesdon.

The Mixed Forplesdons take place in impenetrable morning mist every October and is, indeed, the Ladies' and Gentlemen's Championship. It imposes a fearful strain on the gallantry of the Gents, most of whom wouldn't dream of playing with Ladies in the ordinary way.

Some of the Ladies, of course, could beat a large number of the Gents using one club only, but the frailer and prettier ones need a lot of nursing.

I was playing, on this occasion, with a prettier and frailer one called Jennifer, Sue or Prue. She was attended by three familiars—ladies of mature years with blue rinses, cashmere sweaters, ghillie shoes and a single strand of pearls. One of them was probably her mother.

On the first couple of greens Jennifer, Sue or Prue never got anywhere near the hole with her putter, for reasons which I couldn't quite analyse. She played a smooth, flowing stroke which looked particularly effective from the back—though my analysis from this angle was terminated on the third by a pointed clearing of the throat from Mummy—but none of them ever looked like dropping, even from a yard away.

Walking down the fourth fairway I asked her if she would like me to help her in deciding the line to the hole.

"I'm frightfully sorry," said Jennifer, Sue or Prue—a polite girl—"it's not that. It's just that—just that—"

"Go on," I said. "You can tell me."

"Well," she said—she was very nervous—"it's just that sometimes I feel that the head of the putter sort of starts back on its own and it's going to climb up the shaft and bite me, so I have to sort of swish it gently down before it can—"

It was a fearful aberration, its vividness increased by its very complexity. I tried to put it right out of my mind.

At the short hole—the one over the lake—Jennifer, Sue or Prue played a splendid tee-shot, despite the intervention of one of those moorhens which always decide to leave home in a hurry just as you're starting your downswing. She left me on the back edge of the green, about ten feet above the hole.

As I advanced to deal with it I saw the late and very great Bernard Darwin perched on his shooting-stick nearby, making notes for his report to *The Times*. Some years before, when Rossall had first achieved the final in the Halford Hewitt at Deal, he had given me a brief mention as—"the big man with the velvet putting touch"—a felicity which I could not have invented or even considered to be relevant myself.

I gave him a grave nod, becoming to a big man with a velvet putting touch about to velvet in a ten-footer for a two.

A preliminary survey revealed that the touch would have to be velvety indeed if I were not to knock Jennifer, Sue or Prue right back into the pond. Ten feet downhill all the way, and the green looking suddenly like glass.

I was shaping up to velvet it when there flashed into my mind, as clearly as though I were looking at it on a cinema screen, the spectacle of the club-head slowly and

menacingly curling back to rise vertically into the air like a striking cobra, and bite me in the hand.

I must have swung the club-head back two feet, to keep the fanged head down. The ball sped straight over the hole and finished perhaps twelve yards away, well out of the range of Jennifer's snake. Our opponents, taking only three putts, won that one easily with, in all probability, several shots in hand.

Mr. Darwin returned my grave nod as we left the green. There was no mention of our match next day in *The Times*.

But how, the anxious novice may well enquire, with the ball changing shape and the putter writhing about, is it ever possible to scuffle one into the hole?

A good question, and I'm glad it was asked, because I found the answer only the other day.

Place the weight on the left leg, with the feet close together and the right one drawn back an inch or two.

Rest the left hand on the thigh.

Move the club-head back using only the wrists.

Bring it down again by the same method.

Follow through as far as the anchored left wrist will let the club-head go.

It doesn't often put them into the hole but it has the appearance of being a solid and dependable method, and this in putting is everything.

Once, I came upon Henry Longhurst on the practice green at Moortown. It was getting dark, but he had his putter out and was playing shots with extreme concentration without, however, using a ball.

My offer to lend him one was rejected out of hand. He was, it seemed, partnering Henry Cotton and had become convinced, quite suddenly, that next day, on the very last green, he would be faced with the situation of having to hole an eight-foot putt to win his distinguished professional partner several hundreds of pounds.

"There will be," said Henry Longhurst, "no earthly chance of my getting it in. I am merely trying now to devise a method which will look as though I must have holed a lot of eight-footers in the past. That is the important thing."

Good putting, therefore, and never mind about the hole. It's bound to get in the way now and then.

11

THE BIG, BIG TIME

In 1949 the British Amateur Championship was played at Portmarnock, Eire—an interesting occasion in view of the fact that the British competitors had to submit to the rigours of passport examination and Customs inspection before being allowed to play in their own championship.

It was—making the situation slightly worse—won by an Irishman, Max Macready, from an American, Willie Turnesa, but what causes the event to linger in my memory is the fact that I got as far as the fifteenth hole in the fifth round—a 300% improvement on all previous endeavours.

Having emigrated, like 920,000 other Irishmen, to England I was drawn to return home for this particular Amateur by the enormous advantage of being able to stay with my parents while it was in progress, and not in an hotel.

Hotels are murder during a championship week if you're not a member of the regular tournament mob. Unless you know—as the English, whose spiritual home is the Armed Forces, say—the drill, you're liable to find yourself shacked up with seven old ladies in a temperance

HOW TO BECOME A SCRATCH GOLFER

guest house ten miles away from the course on which the championship is being played.

On all these occasions there is always one hotel in which the knowledgeable boys are gathered together, and if you're not in it it promotes an emotional climate in which you're already three down.

There are no means of assessing—say from the A.A. book—which this hotel is likely to be. Choose the four-star one and you find that all the boys are staying at half the price in a charming road-house immediately opposite the course. If the four-star hotel is the right one you can only get into it by booking a month ahead, before you've seen the draw. When you do see the draw, and find you've got Joe Carr in the first round, a reservation for five days at £3. 10s. per day bed and breakfast looks like being an unnecessary expense.

The night life of hotels can draw you out very fine, too. After dinner you can sit in the lounge on the outskirts of the knowledgeable boys listening to them talking about Amateurs they have taken part in in the past. There is no limit to the scope or the accuracy of their reminiscences. They can recount, shot by shot, the details of every round they've played over the last five years, with sidelights on the exceptional good fortune, in moments of crisis, enjoyed by other distinguished players who beat them at Deal, Troon, Hoylake and everywhere else. Attempts by the non-tournament man to introduce subjects of a more general nature, like the plays of Ionescu, Picasso's ceramics or the convoluted literary style of Henry James meet with no success.

The alternative is to go to bed and get a good night's

sleep, to be alert and fresh for the morrow. But before retiring it's obviously a good idea to get out the putter, and knock a few balls up and down the carpet.

There's a design of stripes on the carpet which, by a happy coincidence, clearly demonstrates whether or not the club-head is being taken back, and brought forward, square to the line of the tooth mug which has been placed on the floor in the opposite corner of the room. But, according to the stripes on the carpet, the club-head is coming back *outside* the line, while the follow-through finishes several inches to the left of the tooth mug, and must, indeed, have been doing so for years. It's still, however, only 9.15. There's ample time to work on it—

By 10 p.m. you're getting only one in six into the tooth mug, against a previous average as high as three. Also, the carpet is much faster than the greens are likely to be. You achieve the conviction that you're practising a putting stroke which will not only push it six inches to the right of the hole every time, but also leave it at least two yards short. Throw the putter back into the bag and get into bed and try to forget all about the stripes. Try, indeed, not to think about golf at all—

Five minutes later you're up, in bare feet and pyjamas, in front of the full-length mirror in the wardrobe, trying to see what it looks like if you really do pull the left hand *down* from the top of the swing, instead of shoving the right shoulder round. Suddenly, it feels right so you get the driver out of the bag and have a swish with it in front of the mirror and it demolishes an alabaster bowl concealing the light fitting in the ceiling. Clear it up and

back into bed and try to think of some reasonable explanation for the chambermaid in the morning—

By midnight there's been another putting session—disastrous—and a spell of short chips into the wastepaper basket two of which, striking the door high up with an incredibly loud bang, provoked a thunderous and outraged knocking on the wall from the man next door. Back into bed—the feet are frozen—where you lie with the sheet up to the eyes wondering if the whole hotel has been roused and the manager, in his dressing-gown, will soon be in with a policeman, and they'll find you've smashed the alabaster bowl and knocked all the paint off the door and there's no explanation. None, except perhaps that you're playing in the Championship—or at it.

To sleep, perchance—except that it's an odds-on certainty—to dream. It's that very special nightmare, unhinging in its grinding frustration, of being on the first tee in the British Amateur Championship, except that the tee is enclosed by a small wooden shed and you're inside it and there's no room for your back-swing and in any case the tee-shot, supposing you could hit it, has got to emerge through a tiny window high up near the roof—

Stark, staring awake and the time is five to five. Get up and have a bath? It might be so weakening that the driver will fly out of your hand and blind Willie Turnesa. Read? The more interesting passages in *Lady Chatterley's Lover* would have the impact of *Eric, Or Little By Little*.

Perhaps the greens are as fast as—much faster than—the carpet. Has anyone, in the Amateur, ever taken four putts on each of the first nine holes?

If the quick hooking starts will six new balls be enough?

HOW TO BECOME A SCRATCH GOLFER

Has anyone, in the Amateur, ever had to *buy* a ball off his opponent as early as the third hole? Is it allowed by the rules . . . ?

The waiters are still laying the tables when you come down to breakfast, and the papers haven't arrived. To spread the meal out—it's only 7.30 a.m.—you order grapefruit, porridge, a kipper, bacon and eggs, coffee, toast and marmalade. Each item goes to join the previous one in what feels like a hot croquet-ball, lodged at the base of the throat.

The chambermaid does want to know what happened to the alabaster light fitting.

The car, left outside all night because the hotel garage is full, won't start.

The contestant for the British Amateur title is ready to —and does—go down without a struggle to a nineteen-year old medical student from Glasgow University, pulling his own trolley, six and five.

For the 1949 Amateur, however, I not only had the comforting presence of my nearest and dearest around me after dark, to say nothing of free board and lodging, but also the benefit of the advice and counsel of Henry Longhurst, who was staying with us.

He was early in the field both with counsel and advice. Before going over to Portmarnock for the first round I had an hour loosening up at a course near my father's house, with Henry in attendance to see, even at this eleventh hour, if something couldn't be done to put things right.

At the end of the first fusillade he said, through clenched teeth, "It's like watching a man scraping a knife against a pewter plate."

Put out—some of them had finished on the fairway—I asked him to be more precise about his discomfort.

"You're trying to hit them round corners," he said. "It's agony to watch it."

We conducted an interesting experiment. I stood up to the ball. Henry laid a club on the ground behind me, pointing in the direction which my stance suggested might be the eventual line of flight. When I came round to have a look I found to my surprise that I'd been aiming at a small shelter in the distance, perhaps fifty yards to the right of the true objective. "Swivel the whole gun round," said Coach, "and try firing one straight."

It seemed madness to tamper with the system now, and specially to try hitting one straight after years of hooking it back from the rough on the right. I tried it, however, just once. Aiming, it seemed to me, diagonally across the fairway to the left, I hit one straight down the middle, quail-high and all, perhaps, of a quarter of a mile.

"Right," said Coach. "We'll leave it at that. You've probably only got four more of those left."

It looked as though four would be enough. My section of the draw was infested with Americans, mostly from Winged Foot—a distinction which suggested that they were all probably well above Walker Cup standard. I'd drawn someone called Udo Reinach, a threatening set of syllables presenting a picture of a crew-cut, All-American tackle weighing 210 lb. with a tee-shot like a naval gun. To remain with Udo for as many as twelve holes would surely see duty done.

I met him. He turned out to be Willie Turnesa's patron and protector who, as he said himself, had just come along for the ride. He was small and elderly and noticeably frail. In a ding-dong struggle, with no quarter given or asked, I beat him on the seventeenth by holing a long, up-hill putt which went off some time before I was ready for it. If we'd completed the course both would have been round in the middle eighties.

Next day I met another American, also from Winged Foot. I've never been able to remember his name, but he was a friend of Udo's. Indeed, he'd known Udo for nearly forty years, which put him in the late sixties. He confessed to me that he had no serious intentions about the Championship at all, having merely come along on the ride that Udo was on, and—owing to a latent heart condition—rather doubted his capacity to get round the whole of Portmarnock's 7,000 yards.

He very nearly had to. I beat him with a four on the seventeenth by putting a 5-iron absolutely stiff after hitting my tee-shot straight along the ground.

It was gratifying to see a line in one of the Dublin evening papers: "In the lower half of the draw Campbell, a local player, is steadily working his way through the American menace."

By the following evening I'd got through another round. I can't remember his name either, but I know he was a Dublin man who was about half my size and capable of playing, on the very top of his game, to a handicap in the region of nine. Coach summed up the situation at dinner that night. "No one," he said, "since the inauguration of the Amateur has ever had it easier for the first three rounds. It's a pity, in a way, it's over now."

He was referring, graciously, to the fact that I was to

meet Billy O'Sullivan in the morning, in the fourth round.

Billy, who was well known to me, had been Irish Amateur Champion so often that it didn't seem possible he hadn't turned pro. With a two-handed, blacksmith's grip he hit it farther off the tee than anyone in Ireland. A Killarney man himself, he'd brought two-thirds of that fiercely partisan area with him, to assist in the laying waste to the city of Dublin which would automatically follow his almost certain victory in the final on Saturday afternoon.

I was devoid of hope. My coach—creator with Valentine Castlerosse of the Killarney Golf Club—had transferred his loyalties without equivocation to the local man, even inviting me to share his pleasure in contemplation of the beating that Billy, with his fine, free, slashing Killarney swing, would hand out to the plodding, mechanical, American methods of Willie Turnesa. "We want him fresh," were my coach's last words of advice, "so don't keep him out there too long—not that you will."

By the eleventh hole it looked as though Billy would be back in the club-house for a long and leisured lunch. He was four up, and on a loose rein. I was aiming the gun right out over the head of mid-wicket and hauling it so far back around the corner that time after time it finished up in the sandhills on the left. We were unattended by an audience. Even the camp-followers from Killarney were drinking stout in the bar, preparing themselves for the rigours of the O'Sullivan-Turnesa final.

Abruptly—and I can't remember how—Billy came to pieces. I got two holes back, so that on the fourteenth tee he was two up with five to go, a margin still sufficiently large, it seemed to me, not to leave the result in doubt.

Then something extraordinary happened. The fourteenth is a long, narrow green sloping up into the sandhills, with several cavernous bunkers in front. You couldn't play short and if you were over you'd a vile, slippery chip all down-hill on a green burnt brown and ten miles an hour faster than any hotel carpet. On the left, however, pin-high, was a patch of short rough into which I'd hooked all three previous second shots, by accident. They had remained there, however, leaving a comparatively simple scuffle up to the hole.

It would, if nothing else, be interesting to see if I could put it into the rough on purpose. For the first time—not having dared to try the innovation before—I swivelled the gun, played left of the green and it stayed there, a combination of almost unbelievable circumstances.

Billy, outside me as usual, played a beautiful iron shot which hit the middle of the green, ran up the slope and disappeared over the top edge. His chip back slid eight feet past. He missed the putt. I holed a shortish one for a four, to be only one down. Even in the white-hot glow of having played a hole with the loaf, and having seen Billy making the obvious mistake, I still regarded it merely as a postponement of the inevitable three and two defeat that was coming my way—particularly in view of the nature of the fifteenth.

It's a short hole—about 170 yards—from a raised tee on the edge of the beach to a green sunk in sandhills, with jungle country all round and a deep hollow on the left. A brisk breeze was blowing off the sea, straight across. A further assurance of disaster was provided by the presence of Laddie Lucas and, I think—my eyesight was beginning to go—Gerald Micklem, an expert audience ready to enjoy to the full a high, looping hook which would not be seen again or, alternatively, a furtive, defensive socket onto the beach.

One—or both—of them remarked that they were glad to see I'd got so far, in view of the fact that rumour had it we'd been back in the club-house for quite some time. No disarmingly modest response occurred to me. An uncontrollable but still faint trembling had started in my legs, more or less guaranteeing a shank. I struck at it quickly with a 3-iron. It travelled low and straight into the crosswind, and finished six-feet from the hole. Incredulous laughter, instantly and graciously muffled, broke from Messrs. Lucas and Micklem. Billy, holding his too far up into the wind, finished on the right-hand edge. His putt was short. Playing for a certain half from six-feet, I put mine into the hole, and we were all square. As we walked down to the sixteenth tee Billy, possibly echoing a thought put into his mind by Lucas and Micklem, made his first remark for some time. "I don't know how you do it," he said.

I couldn't have told him, even if he'd really wanted to know. I was too busy trying to think of a method, based upon past experience, which would put my tee-shot on the fairway, and at least 200 yards away. The sixteenth is a long par-5, and grouped around the distant green were something like five hundred people, waiting for the close finishes. For reasons of personal dignity and self-respect I had no desire to intrude into their company, having already played four.

The knee-trembling was becoming more acute, very similar, in fact, to the time when as a child of ten I was menaced by armed members of the I.R.A. My only desire was that the match should be over, one way or the other. No trace of the killer instinct had established itself, although I'd won four holes in a row.

It felt like a fairly good one, though the follow-through was curtailed because long after I'd hit it I was still looking at the ground. It turned out to have been low and rather hooky, but on the hard ground it had gone quite a long way. Billy hit a rasper right down the middle.

Then, as we walked off the tee, we saw an extraordinary thing—a spectacle like an infantry regiment, charging towards us. It was the five hundred people—probably two hundred of them from Killarney—who'd been waiting round the green. Instinct seemed to have warned them that a Homeric struggle—I was thinking like a golf correspondent—was in progress, and they wanted to be in on the kill.

They engulfed us. I lost sight of Billy, over to the right. I became conscious of an excited steward, dragging a length of rope. "Jaysus—" he cried—"I never thought I'd be doin' this for you!" He put down the rope and I stepped over it. "Get back there!" he bawled at the crowd. "Back there now, an' give him room!"

The ball was lying just on the edge of the rough, but nicely cocked up. People were standing round it in a semi-circle, five deep, craning in death-like silence to see over one another's heads. Hundreds more, lining the fairway, made it look like a long, solid tunnel to the green. It had the curious effect of promoting confidence, so many people expecting to see it go straight.

I took a long, slow swing with a 3-wood, making it look right for the audience. There was a lovely whip off the shaft, but I never saw where it went. They were after it, almost before I'd hit it. All I saw was a mass of backs, running away from me. My caddy and I were left alone. He was a young and inexperienced lad, as staggered as I was that we'd got so far. "I never seen a t'ing," he said.

Billy and I were both short, left and right, though I only knew where he was by the crowd around him. Someone told me it was my shot, and asked me the score. I found I didn't know.

I'd a fifty yard chip, up to the hole. Again the crowd, pressing in, seemed to narrow down the possibilities of error. I left it two feet from the hole. Then the running backs hid it from me again, forming a solid, brightly coloured wall round the green. I'd quite a job to push through them, to find that Billy was about four feet away. Both of us holed our putts. Before mine dropped the gallery were running for the next tee.

It was still my honour. The ball was looking dingy and scuffed, after the hard, sandy fairways, but in a peculiar way I felt it was part of me, that it knew what we were trying to do. Nothing could have made me change it for a new one. We were both in this together, and what we were trying to do was to beat hell out of Billy O'Sullivan, for whom I'd suddenly conceived such a hatred that I could scarcely wait to bash one down the middle so far that he'd jump at his and please God leave himself with an unplayable lie in a bush.

We were both down the middle. As I walked slowly and shakily after the running backs, now seemingly multiplied by four, I was accosted by a well-spoken stranger. "Are you all right?" he asked me. He appeared strangely concerned. "Yeah," I said. "Yes." He looked at me for a long moment. "You look," he said, "as if you're going to faint." I saw for the first time that it was my father. "I'm all right," I told him, and walked on.

We were both on in two. We both got our four. We walked in silence to the eighteenth tee—all square and one to go.

It took a long time before the stewards were able to clear the course. It was round about lunch time. People were pouring out of the club-house and the beer tents, running for positions of vantage. In a championship all square and one to go will cause any true golf enthusiast even to put down his bottle of stout, and come out and have a look.

The eighteenth at Portmarnock is a nasty one. A long, high mound on the left means you've got to keep your tee-shot well out on the right, to get a view of the green, and even then there's a rise in front of it which stops you seeing more than the top half of the pin.

I stood up to the ball, still having the honour. All hatred of Billy O'Sullivan had subsided, having given way to a bone-cracking weariness in which whatever mental processes were still alive were focused upon the immediate warming and soothing after-effects of two large Irish whiskeys in one glass.

I was shifting the club-head about, trying to get a grip with the left hand which would push the ball out to the right, away from the mound on the other side, when someone let out a roar that froze me solid. "Fore—" he bawled —"ya silly ole bitch!"

I looked up—and saw an elderly woman, her wits deranged by scores of shouted, contrary instructions, scurrying about in the middle of the fairway, like a rabbit fleeting from two thousand dogs. A friend or relative fell upon her, and dragged her away to safety. I started all over again. A moment later, playing with the greatest care and concentration, I hooked my tee-shot straight into the base of the mound.

"Bad luck," said Billy. It seemed to me that his rugged features were irradiated by an expression of gentle, brotherly love. The swine hit a beauty, a mile long and out on the right, giving him an easy 6-iron to the green.

I was sloping after the running backs again, trying to calculate the minutes that remained between me and the two large Irish, when I found myself confronted by H. Longhurst, my patron and coach, of whom I'd seen nothing during the heat of the day. "You're doing well," he said pleasantly. "Why not try winning, for a change?"

"Go," I told him, "and set them up inside. Plain water with mine." Knowledgeable man that he is, he walked away.

It wasn't lying too badly but, being under the mound, I couldn't see the green. I took out a 5-iron and hit it high into the air. It felt fairly all right, but the gallery put me straight. They let out a great cry of, "Oooh—!" on a descending scale, indicating beyond doubt that we were up to the ears in the radishes, for the first time for six holes.

I'd no idea where it was and still hadn't, when I reached the green, which was hemmed in by the largest crowd I'd ever seen. There was no trace of the ball or, indeed, of anyone who seemed to know where it might be found. I pushed through the people massed in front of me and then heard a disordered shouting away to the left. Someone over there was waving a small red flag on the end of a long pole. I was in a deep bunker so far off the line, and so little used, that it was full of scattered stones and weeds growing up through the sand.

I went in after it. It was lying all right, clear at least of the stones. It was only then that I remembered Billy, and the important part that he was playing in the proceedings. I asked someone what had happened to him. He didn't know. General conjecture and speculation broke out. Several people thought he'd put it stiff. Others believed he was out of bounds, in the garden of the clubhouse. In the middle of all this a man, carrying a ham sandwich and a cardboard glass of stout, came running over the hill, his face suffused with excitement. "He's up to his doodlers in the pot bunker!" he bawled. "Ye've got him cold!"

For the second time, in this last, vital hole, I was about to play a shot without being able to see the pin—a fair commentary, I had time to remark, upon the accuracy of my method under pressure. I climbed out to have a look and saw Billy, already standing in the deep pot bunker cut into the right-hand edge of the green. The pin was only a few yards away from him. He'd have to play a miraculous one to get his four. If I could scuffle mine out and take only two putts, we'd very shortly be starting off down the first again, drawing farther and farther away from the healing malt in the bar.

I climbed down into the bunker again. The only unforgivable thing would be to leave it there. Expelling every breath of air from my lungs that might build up unwanted pressure, I swung the club-head slowly back and equally slowly forward. It nipped the ball rather sweetly. It disappeared over the brow of the hill.

When I pushed through the crowd and walked on to the green I knew at once which was mine. It was four feet from the hole, a not impossible, dead straight putt, slightly up hill. Billy was three or four yards past it. No one could have holed it out of that pot bunker, with a burnt-up green.

He had a horrible curly one with a 6-inch borrow all down the side of the hill. He missed it.

I can remember exactly how I holed mine. I gripped the putter so tightly that it was impossible to break the wrists, and shoved it straight in. So incalculable are the workings of the human mind that I knew, even under that nerve-crinkling pressure, that I couldn't miss.

I don't remember anything at all about the next half-hour. There must have been a great deal of pleasure in assuring people in the bar that I had, in fact, beaten Billy O'Sullivan. The opportunity must have arisen for the extra pleasure of telling them, in part, how. There must also have been the extreme physical joy of the corrosive malt, slowly seeping through the system shaky and dehydrated by tension, fear and the need to discipline muscles jumpy and wayward as jelly. It's all a blur, but I do remember the thing that suddenly gave it edge and

shape. It was the reminder, by someone who'd just bought me another large one, that I had, within the hour, to go out and do it again.

I would like, at this point, to make the frank admission that I knew I hadn't won the Championship by getting through four rounds but, at the same time, that I had reached a state of euphoria in which it practically seemed that I had. That is, to well deserved roars of applause, I'd got much further even than my own mother—a nonplayer—would ever have imagined and now, full of drink and glory, was more than ready to step off the bus. Except that I was still in the Championship, and was off at 2.15, facing the powerful, ruthless and determined Kenneth Thom.

I recall a private moment of agonizing—you can say that again—reappraisal in the convenience section of the gentlemen's locker room. I had to go out again and, stiff, sore, blurred and exhausted, beat Ken Thom. Another one into the rough on the left of the fourteenth, chip up and hole the putt. Another wind-splitter to the short fifteenth, and hole that one too. Then the three long holes home and the feeling of evening coming on and tattered newspaper blowing across the course and the fairways shiny and slippery with the battering of countless feet and cars filled with careless merrymakers driving away down the road because the main excitement of the day is over—except that, to survive, I've still got to get a four at the eighteenth and I'm in behind the mound ...

Another thought occurred to me in the cathedral silence of the convenience section of the gentlemen's locker room. With this next round the Championship proper was only about to begin. The first four rounds, which had brought me to my knees, were in fact only a routine clearing away of the dross—a removal of the cheerful, slap-happy elements who'd merely come along for the ride. From now on we were getting down to work, opening up a little on the tee-shots, really picking the spots, far out, where we could start drilling home those iron-shots, going for our threes. One more round today—and two more tomorrow—*two more tomorrow!*—followed by the 36 hole final—36 HOLES AT THE END OF A WEEK!—after which one of us would step up to receive the trophy, remark that the course seemed to be in excellent condition and that the runner-up had played a really wonderful game—and then, with the whites of the eyes rolling up, keel over backwards and fall stone dead. Except, of course, that the real men who win championships don't have much time to hang around afterwards, dying or making idle remarks. They've got to look slippy and get to the airport, because there are only three days for practice before exactly the same thing begins all over again.

I concluded the agonizing reappraisal, stunned by the size of the suddenly revealed gap between the real men and the lucky mice, and went to have lunch. There was only half an hour left before Ken Thom helped himself to a victory, the ease of which would pleasurably surprise him, at this comparatively late stage.

As soon as I got into the tent I saw that he must have had lunch already. Or, perhaps, a prey—wholly unjustifiably—to tournament nerves, he'd decided to leave it out altogether. The wind had increased in severity. Every time it blew back the flap of the lunch tent I could see him in the distance on the practice ground. With a whiplash crack he was drilling iron shots into the teeth of the wind under the expert instruction of the late Fred Robson, although I can't imagine what either of them were worrying about. All they had to do, if they were anxious about being beaten, was to come into the tent and watch me trying to wash down a lobster salad with alternative draughts of Guinness and John Jameson, a menu chosen more or less at random.

There was nothing left in the horse. Indeed, so little competitive spirit remained that I remember nothing whatever of the fifth and final round, except for the incident at the second hole.

Ken won the first—I think with a shaky five which wasn't, however, threatened at any point. At the next, I was miles away in the long, tenacious grass on the left. A

clump with an 8-iron failed to do it very much harm, apart from improving the lie. I put the next one on the green, and left it on the lip of the hole for a five.

Ken already had his four. He knocked my ball away. "Half," he said. As we walked to the next tee, having rejected the undesirable solution of charity, I decided he hadn't seen the abortive bash with the 8-iron, presumed I was on in two and might even be counting himself lucky that my long putt hadn't gone in for a birdie.

Some light shadow-boxing took place with my conscience which, however, was in no shape for a major contest. I was storing the incident away in my bottom drawer, with plenty of old clothes on top of it to keep it away from the light, when I found Coach once more by my side. "Well played," he said, with apparently genuine admiration. "A couple more of those and you'll beat him."

It proved a confusing spur. I was still only one down after four more holes, though in reality, of course, it was two. On the fifth tee I had a night—or day—mare. Suppose by some inconceivable chance I had another resurrection and holed a four-footer on the eighteenth, to win one-up, would it then be possible to walk over to Ken Thom and in the presence of 5,000 people tell him that he'd got his arithmetic all trollocked up on the second and in fact we were still all-square? And how would Ken Thom, a dark, thick-set and dour young man, take it? What he'd do would be to concede the match, on the grounds that it was his own fault, and I'd have to get down on my knees in the middle of the eighteenth green and beg him to reconsider his quixotic decision. He'd turn away from this pitiful snivelling and the gallery would start throwing ham sandwiches, shooting-sticks, umbrellas . . .

The matter did not arise, nor did it ever look as if it would. Ken Thom won far out in the country, counting—probably having been tipped off by one of his supporters who'd seen the incident at the second—every one of the

shower of sixes that turned out to be the best that I could do in the fifth round of the Amateur Championship, when all of us were opening the tap a bit and really starting to go for those threes.

At this late stage it seems improbable that I shall have another shot at the Amateur title.

You've got to qualify now before you're allowed in.